Book of Adam and Eve
Illustrated Edition

**From "The Apocrypha and Pseudepigrapha
of the Old Testament"
R.H. Charles
1913**

Reprint 2011

U.S.A.

ZuuBooks specialize in offering rare printed and ebooks for affordable prices. For more information on our products and services for authors please contact us at ilifeebooks@gmail.com

This has been a ZuuBooks.com Publication. For New and Classic titles in Audiobooks, ebooks, and Paperback please visit us at www.zuuBooks.com

Authors who are interested in publishing and distributing their works can contact us at ilifeebooks@gmail.com

Book of Adam and Eve

Illustrated Edition

**From "The Apocrypha and Pseudepigrapha
of the Old Testament"
R.H. Charles
1913**

Reprint 2011

U.S.A.

PREFACE

TODAY the medley of outward life has made a perplexity of inward life. We moderns have ruffled our old incertitudes to an absurd point--incertitudes that are older than theology.

Not without justification have priests mounted altars for generations and cried, "Oh my soul, why dost thou trouble me?"

We are active, restless both in body and mind. Curiosity has replaced blind faith. We go groping, peering, searching, scornful of dogmas, back, further back to sources. And just as the physicist thrills at the universes he discovers as he works inward in the quest of his electrons, so the average man exults in his apprehension of fundamentals of psychology. New cults spring up, attesting to the Truth--as they see it--countless fleets of Theism, Buchmanism, Theosophy, Bahai'ism, etc., sail under brightly colored flags; and Atheism is flaunting itself on the horizon.

Almost the passengers have turned pilots. Everyman is thinking for himself.

The findings here--in this strange volume--bring the reader into a large inland sea, cut off from the traffic and the tempest that have sprung up in the West; and untouched by the crosscurrents of dogmas and presumptions that have cluttered historic centuries. Here is virgin water that gushes, troubled by abysmal forces only, out of the very earth itself.

Whence are these writings--these emotions--these profound pages of wisdom? You might as well inquire, whence is human nature? The fact is--they are. It isn't as though you can compare this literature with any other, as you might compare the French Romanticists with the Russian school. If you do so, this man may say it is too fantastic; that man, it is too coarse; the other man, it is too "out of date"! And they straightway lose all sight of the fact that it is simply fundamental.

To be sure scholars will argue, and inquire. They would find the exact history; the shape of this or that Greek stem; they would set the opinion of this erudite authority against the opinion of that. It is right that they, as scholars, should do so. It is right that the average man who is not a scholar should also do so-if he wants to; and should not have to do so, if he does not want to.

It is, however, only just to pay a tribute to scholarship which has preceded and made possible this book. The publishers are indispensably indebted to The

Apocrypha and Pseudepigrapha edited by R. H. Charles, D. Litt., D. D.; The Odes and Psalms of Solomon by Dr. Rendel Harris; The Book of Adam and Eve by the Rev. S. C. Malan, D. D., published in England in 1882.

*   *   *   *

It is appropriate to leave this book in your hands with the invocation of San Peladan, which Conrad has translated for us. San Pelandan believed in astrology, spirits of the air, elves, nymphs and everything that is deliciously fantastic. However, he did say:

"O Nature, indulgent Mother, forgive! Open your arms to the son, prodigal and weary.

"I have attempted to tear asunder the veil you have hung to conceal from us the pain of life, and I have been wounded by the mystery. . . . Oedipus, half way to finding the word of the enigma, young Faust, regretting already the simple life, the life of the heart, I come back to you repentant, reconciled, O gentle deceiver!"

*   *   *   *

Adam and Eve; Solomon; Pharaoh; Aristeas; Ahikar; and the Twelve Intellectual Giants--we come back to you.

R. H. P. JR.

New York, August I, 1927.

INTRODUCTION

By WILLIAM N. GUTHRIE, D.D.

 Rector of St. Mark's-in-the-Bouwerie.

AN American Indian's Song is his very own. No other man can sing it without his explicit permission. It is impregnate with his aura. It is not in our sense, however, property. It is believed to invest magically the singer with the mood whence it proceeded, and must, therefore, merge in some way the performer's identity with that of the originator's. To sing another's song is an invasion of his personality, a sort of spiritual piracy involving sacrilege.

When last year in Arcady and Andritzena, I induced primitive shepherds to sing and play for me lustily all sorts of occasional songs and rituals, they refused to do a burial chant, most positively. For to perform one would surely cause a death in the house.

A little reflection on these two paragraphs may perhaps, make the reader realize that authorship was once a thing of great hazards. If one had something great and new to say, and wanted it to circulate widely, one would naturally prefer anonymity.

Indeed, by the Hebrews a story was popularly presumed to have its hero for its author. Moses wrote the account of his own death. Deuteronomy was of course, his own work, although obviously intended to alter the traditional religion. Jonah wrote the little novel about himself. David was the author of the Psalms because reported to have instituted the first temple choir, and as a lad to have played the harp soothing the nerves of King Saul. When an author for the book of Job was wanted, though the whole discussion of the work proves it was written to refute the Wisdom literature which by tradition began with the Proverbs of Solomon, Moses was chosen as a suitable author!

So for centuries among the Jews, writers sought to shelter themselves behind the names of the great dead. In this they were guilty of no fraud. They imagined what Solomon or Enoch would say, or sing, upon a particular theme under given circumstances. It was not really they themselves, but their Solomon, their Enoch, Solomon or Enoch in them, who uttered the new prophesies or temple praises.

Thus arose that body of literature, called by modern scholars, "Pseudepigrapha," that is, writings erroneously, unhistorical, and yet sincerely, ascribed to heroic figures summed from the vasty deep by a self-denying imagination, eager to alter man's belief and custom, to interpret his hope and sorrow, without personal gain or fame, and also, may one add, without the deterrent of persecution to arrest free utterance!

Now it is a foolish modern prejudice against an ancient piece of literature that its author veiled his person in this fashion. The only question is: Was the writing of inherent value? Did it exercise influence?

It is not too much to say that no modern can intelligently understand the New Testament, unless he is acquainted with the so-called "Apocrypha," and with the "Pseudepigrapha" as well. The very words of Jesus were in many instances, suggested by sayings current in his day, more or less as unconscious quotations from the Testaments of the 12 Patriarchs.

The figure of the Messiah which Jesus adapted to his creative purpose, cannot be imagined by a modern without a perusal of the book of Enoch which is its classic and most entrancing glorification. Without the Odes and Songs of Solomon the atmosphere breathed by the earliest church cannot be divined.

Hitherto access to this literature has been confined to technical scholars. Its assembly would require special information and considerable expenditure. With this enterprise of the Alpha House, Inc., it becomes democratic property. We shall have a more intelligent clergy and laity, when this volume has taken its place in every library, and is familiarly brought into every discussion of the historic Christ and of His times.

THE FIRST BOOK OF

Adam and Eve

ALSO CALLED

The Conflict of Adam and Eve with Satan.

PRESENT day controversy that rages around the authenticity of the Scriptures and how human life began on this planet must pause to consider the Adam and Eve story. Where does it come from? What does it mean?

The familiar version in Genesis is not the source of this fundamental legend, it is not a spontaneous, Heaven-born account that sprang into place in the Old Testament. It is simply a version, unexcelled perhaps, but a version of a myth or belief or account handed down by word of mouth from generation to generation of mankind-through the incoherent, unrecorded ages of man it came--like an inextinguishable ray of light that ties the time when human life began, with the time when the human mind could express itself and the human hand could write.

This is the most ancient story in the world--it has survived because it embodies the basic fact of human life. A fact that has not changed one iota; amid all the superficial changes of civilization's vivid array, this fact remains: the conflict of Good and Evil; the fight between Man and the Devil; the eternal struggle of human nature against sin,

That the Adam and Eve story pervaded the thoughts of ancient writers is seen in the large number of versions that exist, or whose existence may be traced, through the writings of Greeks, Syrians, Egyptians, Abyssinians, Hebrews, and other ancient peoples. As a lawyer might say who examines so much apparently unrelated evidence--there must be something back of it.

The version which we give here is the work of unknown Egyptians (the lack of historical allusion makes it impossible to date the writing). Parts of this version are found in the Talmud, the Koran, and elsewhere, showing what a vital role it played in the original literature of human wisdom. The Egyptian author first wrote in Arabic (which may be taken as the original manuscript) and that found its way farther south and was translated into Ethiopic. For the present English translation we are indebted to Dr. S. C. Malan, Vicar of Broadwindsor, who worked from the Ethiopic edition edited by Dr. E. Trumpp, Professor at the University of Munich.

Dr. Trumpp had the advantage of the Arabic original, which makes our bridge over the gap of many centuries a direct one.

The reading of these books is an adventure. You will find the mind of man fed by the passions, hopes, fears of new and strange earthly existence rioting, unrestrained, in the zest of self-expression. You roam in the realms of mythology where swiftly the aspects of nature assume manifold personalities, and the amorphous instinct of sin takes on the grotesqueries of a visible devil.

From such imaginative surroundings you find yourself suddenly staring at commonplace unvarnished events of family life--and such a family as "the first earthly family" was! They had all the troubles, all the petty disagreements, and the taking sides with one another, and the bother moving, and "staying with the baby," that in the total mark family life to-day. You will see it when you peep beneath the overlaying glamour of tradition.

One critic has said of this writing:

"This is we believe, the greatest literary discovery that the world has known. Its effect upon contemporary thought in molding the judgment of the future generations is of incalculable value.

"The treasures of Tut-ank-Amen's Tomb were no more precious to the Egyptologist than are these literary treasures to the world of scholarship."

But we prefer to let the reader make his own exploration and form his own opinion. The writing is arresting enough to inspire very original thoughts concerning it,

In general, this account begins where the Genesis story of Adam and Eve leaves off. Thus the two can not well be compared; here we have a new chapter--a sort of sequel to the other. Here is the story of the twin sisters of Cain and Abel, and it is notable that here the blame for the first murder is placed squarely at the door of a difference over Woman.

The plan of these books is as follows:--

Book I. The careers of Adam and Eve, from the day they left Eden; their dwelling in the Cave of Treasures; their trials and temptations; Satan's manifold apparitions to them. The birth of Cain, of Abel, and of their twin sisters; Cain's love for his own twin sister, Luluwa, whom Adam and Eve wished to join to Abel; the details of Cain's murder of his brother; and Adam's sorrow and death.

Book IL The history of the patriarchs who lived before the Flood; the dwelling of the children of Seth on the Holy Mountain--Mount Hermon--until they were lured by Henun and by the daughters of Cain, to come' down from the mountain. Cain's death, when slain by Lamech the blind; and the lives of other patriarchs until the birth of Noah.

BOOK I.

CHAP. I.

The crystal sea. God commands Adam, expelled from Eden, to dwell in the Cave of Treasures.

ON the third day, God planted the garden in the east of the earth, on the border of the world eastward, beyond which, towards the sun-rising, one finds nothing but water, that encompasses the whole world, and reaches unto the borders of heaven.

2 And to the north of the garden there is a sea of wafer, clear and pure to the taste, like unto nothing else; so that, through the clearness thereof, one may look into the depths of the earth.

3 And when a man washes himself in it, becomes clean of the cleanness thereof, and white of its whiteness--even if he were dark.

4 And God created that sea of His own good pleasure, for He knew what would come of the man He should make; so that after he had left the garden, on account of his transgression, men should be born in the earth, from among whom righteous ones should die, whose souls God would raise at the last day; when they should return to their flesh; should bathe in the water of that sea, and all of them repent of their sins.

5 But when God made Adam go out of the garden, He did not place him on the border of it northward, lest he should draw near to the sea of water, and he and Eve wash themselves in it, be cleansed from their sins, forget the transgression they had committed, and he no longer reminded of it in the thought of their punishment.

6 Then, again, as to the southern side of the garden, God was not pleased to let Adam dwell there; because, when the wind blew from the north, it would bring him, on that southern side, the delicious smell of the trees of the garden.

7 Wherefore God did not put Adam there, lest he should smell the sweet smell of those trees forget his transgression, and find consolation for what he had done, take delight in the smell of the trees, and not be cleansed from his transgression.

8 Again, also, because God is merciful and of great pity, and governs all things in a way He alone knows--He made our father Adam dwell in the western border of the garden, because on that side the earth is very broad.

9 And God commanded him to dwell there in a cave in a rock--the Cave of Treasures below the garden.

CHAP. II.

Adam and Eve faint upon leaving the Garden. God sends His word to encourage them.

BUT when our father Adam, and Eve, went out of the garden, they trod the ground on their feet, not knowing they were treading.

2 And when they came to the opening of the gate of the garden, and saw the broad earth spread before them, covered with stones large and small, and with sand, they feared and trembled, and fell on their faces, from the fear that came upon them; and they were as dead.

3 Because--whereas they had hitherto been in the garden-land, beautifully planted with all manner of trees--they now saw themselves, in a strange land, which they knew not, and had never seen.

4 And because at that time they were filled with the grace of a bright nature, and they had not hearts turned towards earthly things.

5 Therefore had God pity on them; and when He saw them fallen before the gate of the garden, He sent His Word unto father Adam and Eve, and raised them from their fallen state.

CHAP. III.

Concerning the promise of the great five days and a half.

GOD said to Adam, "I have ordained on this earth days and years, and thou and thy seed shall dwell and walk in it, until the days and years are fulfillled; when I shall send the
Word that created thee, and against which thou hast transgressed, the Word that made thee come out of the garden and that raised thee when thou wast fallen.

2 Yea, the Word that will again save thee when the five days and a half are fulfillled."

3 But when Adam heard these words from God, and of the great five days and a half, he did not understand the meaning of them.

4 For Adam was thinking that there would be but five days and a half for him, to the end of the world.

5 And Adam wept, and prayed God to explain it to him.

6 Then God in His mercy for Adam who was made after His own image and similitude, explained to him, that these were 5,000 and 500 years; and how One would then come and save him and his seed.

7 But God had before that made this covenant with our father, Adam, in the same terms, ere he came out of the garden, when he was by the tree whereof Eve took the fruit and gave it him to eat.

8 Inasmuch as when our father Adam came out of the garden, he passed by that tree, and saw how God had then changed the appearance of it into another form, and how it withered.

9 And as Adam went to it he feared, trembled and fell down; but God in His mercy lifted him up, and then made this covenant with him.

10 And, again, when Adam was by the gate of the garden, and saw the cherub with a sword of flashing fire in his hand, and the cherub grew angry and frowned at him, both Adam and Eve became afraid of him, and thought he meant to put them to death. So they fell on their faces, and trembled with fear.

11 But he had pity on them, and showed them mercy; and turning from them went up to heaven, and prayed unto the Lord, and said:--

12 "Lord, Thou didst send me to watch at the gate of the garden, with a sword of fire.

13 "But when Thy servants, Adam and Eve, saw me, they fell on their faces, and were as dead. O my Lord, what shall we do to Thy servants?"

14 Then God had pity on them, and showed them mercy, and sent His Angel to keep the garden.

15 And the Word of the Lord came unto Adam and Eve, and raised them up.

16 And the Lord said to Adam, "I told thee that at the end of five days and a half, I will send my Word and save thee.

17 "Strengthen thy heart, therefore, and abide in the Cave of Treasures, of which I have before spoken to thee."

18 And when Adam heard this Word from God, he was comforted with that which God had told him. For He had told him how He would save him.

CHAP. IV.

Adam laments the changed conditions. Adam and Eve enter the Cave of Treasures.

BUT Adam and Eve wept for having come out of the garden, their first abode.

2 And, indeed, when Adam looked at his flesh, that was altered, he wept bitterly, he and Eve, over what they had done. And they walked and went gently down into the Cave of Treasures.

3 And as they came to it Adam wept over himself and said to Eve, "Look at this cave that is to be our prison in this world, and a place of punishment!

4 "What is it compared with the garden? What is its narrowness compared with the space of the other?

5 "What is this rock, by the side of those groves? What is the gloom of this cavern, compared with the light of the garden?

6 "What is this overhanging ledge of rock to shelter us, compared with the mercy of the Lord that overshadowed us?

7 "What is the soil of this cave compared with the garden-land? This earth, strewed with stones; and that, planted with delicious fruit-trees?"

8 And Adam said to Eve, "Look at thine eyes, and at mine, which afore beheld angels in heaven, praising; and they, too, without ceasing.

9 "But now we do not see as we did: our eyes have become of flesh; they cannot see in like manner as they saw before."

10 Adam said again to Eve, "What is our body to-day, compared to what it was in former days, when we dwelt in the garden?"

11 After this Adam did not like to enter the cave, under the overhanging rock; nor would he ever have entered it.

12 But he bowed to God's orders; and said to himself, "Unless I enter the cave, I shall again be a transgressor."

CHAP. V.

In which Eve makes a noble and emotionable intercession, taking the blame on herself.

THEN Adam and Eve entered the cave, and stood praying, in their own tongue, unknown to us, but which they knew well.

2 And as they prayed, Adam raised his eyes, and saw the rock and the roof of the cave that covered him overhead, so that he could see neither heaven, nor God's creatures. So he wept and smote heavily upon his breast, until he dropped, and was as dead.

3 And Eve sat weeping; for she believed he was dead.

4 Then she arose, spread her hands towards God, suing Him for mercy and pity, and said, "O God, forgive me my sin, the sin which I committed, and remember it not against me.

5 "For I alone caused Thy servant to fall from the garden into this lost estate; from light into this darkness; and from the abode of joy into this prison.

6 "O God, look upon this Thy servant thus fallen, and raise him from his death, that he may weep and repent of his transgression which he committed through me.

7 "Take not away his soul this once; but let him live that he may stand after the measure of his repentance, and do Thy will, as before his death.

8 "But if Thou do not raise him up, then, O God, take away my own soul, that I be like him; and leave me not in this dungeon, one and alone; for I could not stand alone in this world, but with him only.

[16]

9 "For Thou, O God, didst cause a slumber to come upon him, and didst take a bone from his side, and didst restore the flesh in the place of it, by Thy divine power.

10 "And Thou didst take me, the bone, and make me a woman, bright like him, with heart, reason, and speech; and in flesh, like unto his own; and Thou didst make me after the likeness of his countenance, by Thy mercy and power.

11 "O Lord, I and he are one and Thou, O God, art our Creator, Thou are He who made us both in one day.

12 "Therefore, O God, give him life, that he may be with me in this strange land, while we dwell in it on account of our transgression.

13 "But if Thou wilt not give him life, then take me, even me, like him; that we both may die the same day."

14 And Eve wept bitterly, and fell upon our father Adam; from her great sorrow.

CHAP. VI.

God's admonition to Adam and Eve in which he points out how and why they sinned.

BUT God looked upon them; for they had killed themselves through great grief.

2 But He would raise them and comfort them.

3 He, therefore, sent His Word unto them; that they should stand and be raised forthwith.

4 And the Lord said unto Adam and Eve, "You transgressed of your own free will, until you came out of the garden in which I had placed you.

5 "Of your own free will have you transgressed through your desire for divinity, greatness, and an exalted state, such as I have; so that I deprived you of the bright nature in which you then were, and I made you come out of the garden to this land, rough and full of trouble.

6 "If only you had not transgressed My commandment and had kept My law, and had not eaten of the fruit of the tree, near which I told you not to come! And there were fruit trees in the garden better than that one.

7 "But the wicked Satan who continued not in his first estate, nor kept his faith; in whom was no good intent towards Me, and who though I had created him, yet set Me at naught, and sought the Godhead, so that I hurled him down from heaven,-- he it is who made the tree appear pleasant in your eyes, until you ate of it, by hearkening to him.

8 "Thus have you transgressed My commandment, and therefore have I brought upon you all these sorrows.

9 "For I am God the Creator, who, when I created My creatures, did not intend to destroy them. But after they had sorely roused My anger, I punished them with grievous plagues, until they repent.

10 "But, if on the contrary, they still continue hardened in their transgression, they shall be under a curse for ever."

Chap. VII.

The beasts are reconciled.

WHEN Adam and Eve heard these words from God, they wept and sobbed yet more; but they strengthened their hearts in God, because they now felt that the Lord was to them like a father and a mother; and for this very reason, they wept before Him, and sought mercy from Him.

2 Then God had pity on them, and said: "O Adam, I have made My covenant with thee, and I will not turn from it; neither will I let thee return to the garden, until My covenant of the great five days and a half is fulfillled."

3 Then Adam said unto God, "O Lord, Thou didst create us, and make us fit to be in the garden; and before I transgressed, Thou madest all beasts come to me, that I should name them.

4 "Thy grace was then on me; and I named every one according to Thy mind; and Thou madest them all subject unto me.

5 "But now, O Lord God, that I have transgressed Thy commandment, all beasts will rise against me and will devour me, and Eve Thy handmaid; and will cut off our life from the face of the earth.

6 "I therefore beseech Thee, O God, that, since Thou hast made us come out of the garden, and hast made us be in a strange land, Thou wilt not let the beasts hurt us."

7 When the Lord heard these words from Adam, He had pity on him, and felt that he had truly said that the beasts of the field would rise and devour him and Eve, because He, the Lord, was angry with them two on account of their transgression.

8 Then God commanded the beasts, and the birds, and all that moves upon the earth, to come to Adam and to be familiar with him, and not to trouble him and Eve; nor yet any of the good and righteous among their posterity.

9 Then the beasts did obeisance to Adam, according to the commandment of God; except the serpent, against which God was wroth. It did not come to Adam, with the beasts.

CHAP. VIII.

The "Bright Nature" of man is taken away.

THEN Adam wept and said, "O God, when we dwelt in the garden, and our hearts were lifted up, we saw the angels that sang praises in heaven, but now we do not see as we were used to do; nay, when we entered the cave, all creation became hidden from us."

2 Then God the Lord said unto Adam, "When thou wast under subjection to Me, thou hadst a bright nature within thee, and for that reason couldst thou see things afar off. But after thy transgression thy bright nature was withdrawn from thee; and it was not left to thee to see things afar off, but only near at hand; after the ability of the flesh; for it is brutish."

3 When Adam and Eve had heard these words from God, they went their way; praising and worshipping Him with a sorrowful heart.

4 And God ceased to commune with them.

CHAP. IX.

Water from the Tree of Life. Adam and Eve near drowning.

THEN Adam and Eve came out of the Cave of Treasures, and drew near to the garden gate, and there they stood to look at it, and wept for having come away from it.

2 And Adam and Eve went from before the gate of the garden to the southern side of it, and found there the water that watered the garden, from the root of the Tree of Life, and that parted itself from thence into four rivers over the earth.

3 Then they came and drew near to that water, and looked at it; and saw that it was the water that came forth from under the root of the Tree of Life in the garden.

4 And Adam wept and wailed, and smote upon his breast, for being severed from the garden; and said to Eve:--

5 "Why hast thou brought upon me, upon thyself, and upon our seed, so many of these plagues and punishments?"

6 And Eve said unto him, "What is it thou hast seen, to weep and to speak to me in this wise?"

7 And he said to Eve, "Seest thou not this water that was with us in the garden, that watered the trees of the garden, and flowed out thence?

8 "And we, when we were in the garden, did not care about it; but since we came to this strange land, we love it, and turn it to use for our body."

9 But when Eve heard these words from him, she wept; and from the soreness of their weeping, they fell into that water; and would have put an end to themselves in it, so as never again to return and behold the creation; for when they looked upon the work of creation, they felt they must put an end to themselves.

CHAP. X.

Their bodies need water after they leave the Garden.

[22]

THEN God, merciful and gracious, looked upon them thus lying in the water, and nigh unto death, and sent an angel, who brought them out of the water, and laid them on the seashore as dead.

2 Then the angel went up to God, was welcome, and said, "O God, Thy creatures have breathed their last."

3 Then God sent His Word unto Adam and Eve, who raised them from their death.

4 And Adam said, after he was raised, "O God, while we were in the garden we did not require, or care for this water; but since we came to this land we cannot do without it."

5 Then God said to Adam, "While thou wast under My command and wast a bright angel, thou knewest not this water.

6 "But after that thou hast transgressed My commandment, thou canst not do without water, wherein to wash thy body and make it grow; for it is now like that of beasts, and is in want of water."

7 When Adam and Eve heard these words from God, they wept a bitter cry; and Adam entreated God to let him return into the garden, and look at it a second time.

8 But God said unto Adam, "I have made thee a promise; when that promise is fulfillled, I will bring thee back into the garden, thee and thy righteous seed."

9 And God ceased to commune with Adam.

CHAP. XI.

A recollection of the glorious days in the Garden.

THEN Adam and Eve felt themselves burning with thirst, and heat, and sorrow.

2 And Adam said to Eve, "We shall not drink of this water, even if we were to die. O Eve, when this water comes into our inner parts, it will increase our punishments and that of our children, that shall come after us."

3 Both Adam and Eve then withdrew from the water, and drank none of it at all; but came and entered the Cave of Treasures.

4 But when in it Adam could not see Eve; he only heard the noise she made. Neither could she see Adam, but heard the noise he made.

5 Then Adam wept, in deep affliction, and smote upon his breast; and he arose and said to Eve, "Where art thou?"

6 And she said unto him, "Lo, I am standing in this darkness."

7 He then said to her, "Remember the bright nature in which we lived, while we abode in the garden!

8 "O Eve! remember the glory that rested on us in the garden. O Eve! remember the trees that overshadowed us in the garden while we moved among them.

9 "O Eve! remember that while we were in the garden, we knew neither night nor day.
Think of the Tree of Life, from below which flowed the water, and that shed lustre over us! Remember, O Eve, the garden-land, and the brightness thereof!

10 "Think, oh think of that garden in which was no darkness, while we dwelt therein.

11 "Whereas no sooner did we come into this Cave of Treasures than darkness compassed us round about; until we can no longer see each other; and all the pleasure of this life has come to an end."

CHAP. XII.

How darkness came between Adam and Eve.

THEN Adam smote upon his breast, he and Eve, and they mourned the whole night until dawn drew near, and they sighed over the length of the night in Miyazia.

2 And Adam beat himself, and threw himself on the ground in the cave, from bitter grief, and because of the darkness, and lay there as dead.

[24]

3 But Eve heard the noise he made in falling upon the earth. And she felt about for him with her hands, and found him like a corpse.

4 Then she was afraid, speechless, and remained by him.

5 But the merciful Lord looked on the death of Adam, and on Eve's silence from fear of the darkness.

6 And the Word of God came unto Adam and raised him from his death, and opened Eve's mouth that she might speak.

7 Then Adam arose in the cave and said, "O God, wherefore has light departed from us, and darkness come over us? Wherefore dost Thou leave us in this long darkness? Why wilt Thou plague us thus?

8 "And this darkness, O Lord, where was it ere it came upon us? It is such, that we cannot see each other.

9 "For, so long as we were in the garden, we neither saw nor even knew what darkness is. I was not hidden from Eve, neither was she hidden from me, until now that she cannot see me; and no darkness came upon us, to separate us from each other.

10 "But she and I were both in one bright light. I saw her and she saw me. Yet now since we came into this cave, darkness has come upon us, and parted us asunder, so that I do not see her, and she does not see me.

11 "O Lord, wilt Thou then plague us with this darkness?"

CHAP. XIII.

The fall of Adam. Why night and day were created.

THEN when God, who is merciful and full of pity, heard Adam's voice, He said unto him:--

2 "O Adam, so long as the good angel was obedient to Me, a bright light rested on him and on his hosts.

3 "But when he transgressed My commandment, I deprived him of that bright nature, and he became dark.

4 "And when he was in the heavens, in the realms of light, he knew naught of darkness.

5 "But he transgressed, and I made him fall from heaven upon the earth; and it was this darkness that came upon him.

6 "And on thee, O Adam, while in My garden and obedient to Me, did that bright light rest also.

7 "But when I heard of thy transgression, I deprived thee of that bright light. Yet, of My mercy, I did not turn thee into darkness, but I made thee thy body of flesh, over which I spread this skin, in order that it may bear cold and heat.

8 "If I had let My wrath fall heavily upon thee, I should have destroyed thee; and had I turned thee into darkness, it would have been as if I killed thee.

9 "But in My mercy, I have made thee as thou art; when thou didst transgress My commandment, O Adam, I drove thee from the garden, and made thee come forth into this land; and commanded thee to dwell in this cave; and darkness came upon thee, as it did upon him who transgressed My commandment.

10 "Thus, O Adam, has this night deceived thee. It is not to last for ever; but is only of twelve hours; when it is over, daylight will return.

11 "Sigh not, therefore, neither be moved; and say not in thy heart that this darkness is long and drags on wearily; and say not in thy heart that I plague thee with it.

12 "Strengthen thy heart, and be not afraid. This darkness is not a punishment. But, O Adam, I have made the day, and have placed the sun in it to give light; in order that thou and thy children should do your work.

13 "For I knew thou shouldest sin and transgress, and come out into this land. Yet would I not force thee, nor be heard upon thee, nor shut up; nor doom thee through thy fall; nor through thy coming out from light into darkness; nor yet through thy coining from the garden into this land.

14 "For I made thee of the light; and I willed to bring out children of light from thee and like unto thee.

15 "But thou didst not keep one day My commandment; until I had finished the creation and blessed everything in it.

16 "Then I commanded thee concerning the tree, that thou eat not thereof. Yet I knew that Satan, who deceived himself, would also deceive thee.

17 "So I made known to thee by means of the tree, not to come near him. And I told thee not to eat of the fruit thereof, nor to taste of it, nor yet to sit under it, nor to yield to it.

18 "Had I not been and spoken to thee, O Adam, concerning the tree, and had I left thee without a commandment, and thou hadst sinned--it would have been an offence on My part, for not having given thee any order; thou wouldst turn round and blame Me for it.

19 "But I commanded thee, and warned thee, and thou didst fall. So that My creatures cannot blame me; but the blame rests on them alone.

20 "And, O Adam, I have made the day for thee and for thy children after thee, for them to work, and toil therein. And I have made the night for them to rest in it from their work; and for the beasts of the field to go forth by night and seek their food.

21 "But little of darkness now remains, O Adam; and daylight will soon appear."

CHAP. XIV.

The earliest prophecy of the coming of Christ.

THEN Adam said unto God: "O Lord, take Thou my soul, and let me not see this gloom any more; or remove me to some place where there is no darkness."

2 But God the Lord said to Adam, "Verily I say unto thee, this darkness will pass from thee, every day I have determined for thee, until the fulfillment of My covenant; when I will save thee and bring thee back again into the garden, into the abode of light thou longest for, wherein is no darkness. I will bring thee, to it--in the kingdom of heaven."

3 Again said God unto Adam, "All this misery that thou hast been made to take upon thee because of thy transgression, will not free thee from the hand of Satan, and will not save thee.

4 "But I will. When I shall come down from heaven, and shall become flesh of thy seed, and take upon Me the infirmity from which thou sufferest, then the darkness that came upon thee in this cave shall come upon Me in the grave, when I am in the flesh of thy seed.

5 "And I, who am without years, shall be subject to the reckoning of years, of times, of months, and of days, and I shall be reckoned as one of the sons of men, in order to save thee."

6 And God ceased to commune with Adam.

CHAP. XV.

THEN Adam and Eve wept and sorrowed by reason of God's word to them, that they should not return to the garden until the fulfilllment of the days decreed upon them; but mostly because God had told them that He should suffer for their salvation.

CHAP. XVI.

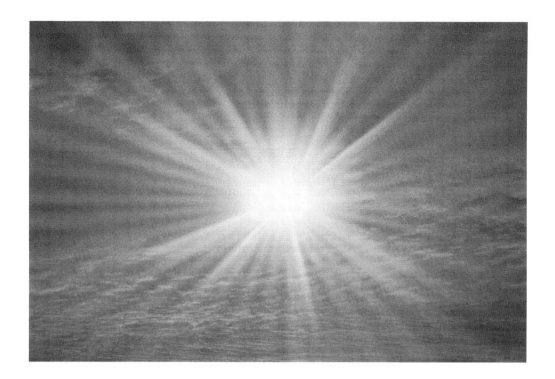

The first sunrise. Adam and Eve think it is a fire coming to burn them.

AFTER this Adam and Eve ceased not to stand in the cave, praying and weeping, until the morning dawned upon them.

2 And when they saw the light returned to them, they restrained from fear, and strengthened their hearts.

3 Then Adam began to come out of the cave. And when he came to the mouth of it, and stood and turned his face towards the east, and saw the sun rise in glowing rays, and felt the heat thereof on his body, he was afraid of it, and thought in his heart that this flame came forth to plague him.

4 He wept then, and smote upon his breast, and fell upon the earth on his face, and made his request, saying:--

5 "O Lord, plague me not, neither consume me, nor yet take away my life from the earth."

6 For he thought the sun was God.

7 Inasmuch as while he was in the garden and heard the voice of God and the sound He made in the garden, and feared Him, Adam never saw the brilliant light of the sun, neither did the flaming heat thereof touch his body.

8 Therefore was he afraid of the sun when flaming rays of it reached him. He thought God meant to plague him therewith all the days He had decreed for him.

9 For Adam also said in his thoughts, as God did not plague us with darkness, behold, He has caused this sun to rise and to plague us with burning heat.

10 But while he was thus thinking in his heart, the Word of God came unto him and said:--

11 "O Adam, arise and stand up. This sun is not God; but it has been created to give light by day, of which I spake unto thee in the cave saying, 'that the dawn would break forth, and there would be light by day.'

12 "But I am God who comforted thee in the night."

13 And God ceased to commune with Adam.

CHAP. XVII.

The Chapter of the Serpent.

THEN Adam and Eve came out at the mouth of the cave, and went towards the garden.

2 But as they drew near to it, before the western gate, from which Satan came when he deceived Adam and Eve, they found the. serpent that became Satan coming at the gate, and sorrowfully licking the dust, and wriggling on its breast on the ground, by reason of the curse that fell upon it from God.

3 And whereas aforetime the serpent was the most exalted of all beasts, now it was changed and become slippery, and the meanest of them all, and it crept on its breast and went on its belly.

4 And whereas it was the fairest of all beasts, it had been changed, and was become the ugliest of them all. Instead of feeding on the best food, now it turned

to eat the dust. Instead of dwelling, as before, in the best places, now it lived in the dust.

5 And, whereas it had been the most beautiful of all beasts, all of which stood dumb at its beauty, it was now abhorred of them.

6 And, again, whereas it dwelt in one beautiful abode, to which all other animals came from elsewhere; and where it drank, they drank also of the same; now, after it had become venomous, by reason of God's curse, all beasts fled from its abode, and would not drink of the water it drank; but fled from it.

CHAP. XVIII.

The mortal combat with the serpent.

WHEN the accursed serpent saw Adam and Eve, it swelled its head, stood on its tail, and with eyes blood-red, did as if it would kill them.

2 It made straight for Eve, and ran after her; while Adam standing by, wept because he had no stick in his hand wherewith to smite the serpent, and knew not how to put it to death.

3 But with a heart burning for Eve, Adam approached the serpent, and held it by the tail; when it turned towards him and said unto him:--

4 "O Adam, because of thee and of Eve, I am slippery, and go upon my belly." Then by reason of its great strength, it threw down Adam and Eve and pressed upon them, as if it would kill them.

5 But God sent an angel who threw the serpent away from them, and raised them up.

6 Then the Word of God came to the serpent, and said unto it, "In the first instance I made thee glib, and made thee to go upon thy belly; but I did not deprive thee of speech.

7 "Now, however, be thou dumb; and speak no more, thou and thy race; because in the first place, has the ruin of my creatures happened through thee, and now thou wishest to kill them."

8 Then the serpent was struck dumb, and spake no more.

9 And a wind came to blow from heaven by command of God that carried away the serpent from Adam and Eve, threw it on the sea shore, and it landed in India.

CHAP. XIX.

 Beasts made subject to Adam.

BUT Adam and Eve wept before God. And Adam said unto Him:--

2 "O Lord, when I was in the cave, I said this to Thee, my Lord, that the beasts of the field would rise and devour me, and cut off my life from the earth."

3 Then Adam, by reason of what had befallen him, smote upon his breast, and fell upon the earth like a corpse; then came to him the Word of God, who raised him, and said unto him,

4 "O Adam, not one of these beasts will be able to hurt thee; because when I made the beasts and other moving things come to thee in the cave, I did not let the serpent come with them, lest it should rise against you, make you tremble; and the fear of it should fall into your hearts.

5 "For I knew that that accursed one is wicked; therefore would I not let it come near you with the other beasts.

6 "But now strengthen thy heart and fear not. I am with thee unto the end of the days I have determined on thee."

CHAP. XX.

 Adam wishes to protect Eve.

THEN Adam wept and said, "O God, remove us to some other place, that the serpent may not come again near us, and rise against us. Lest it find Thy handmaid Eve alone and kill her; for its eyes are hideous and evil."

2 But God said to Adam and Eve, "Henceforth fear not, I will not let it come near you; I have driven it away from you, from this mountain; neither will I leave in it aught to hurt you."

3 Then Adam and Eve worshipped before God 'and gave Him thanks, and praised Him for having delivered them from death.

CHAP. XXI.

Adam and Eve attempt suicide.

THEN Adam and Eve went in search of the garden.

2 And the heat beat like a flame on their faces; and they sweated from the heat, and wept before the Lord.

3 But the place where they wept was nigh unto a high mountain, facing the western gate of the garden.

4 Then Adam threw himself down from the top of that mountain; his face was torn and his flesh was flayed; much blood flowed from him, and he was nigh unto death.

5 Meanwhile Eve remained standing on the mountain weeping over him, thus lying.

6 And she said, "I wish not to live after him; for all that he did to himself was through me."

7 Then she threw herself after him; and was torn and scotched by stones; and remained lying as dead.

8 But the merciful God, who looks upon His creatures, looked upon Adam and Eve as they lay dead, and He sent His Word unto them, and raised them.

9 And said to Adam, "O Adam, all this misery which thou hast wrought upon thyself, will not avail against My rule, neither will it alter the covenant of the 5500 years."

CHAP. XXII.

Adam in a chivalrous mood.

THEN Adam said to God, "I wither in the heat; I am faint from walking, and am loth of this world. And I know not when Thou wilt bring me out of it, to rest."

2 Then the Lord God said unto him, "O Adam, it cannot be at present, not until thou hast ended thy days. Then shall I bring thee out of this wretched land."

3 And Adam said to God, "While I was in the garden I knew neither heat, nor languor, neither moving about, nor trembling, nor fear; but now since I came to this land, all this affliction has come upon me."

4 Then God said to Adam, "So long as thou wast keeping My commandment, My light and My grace rested on thee. But when thou didst transgress My commandment, sorrow and misery befell thee in this land."

5 And Adam wept and said, "O Lord, do not cut me off for this, neither smite me with heavy plagues, nor yet repay me according to my sin; For we, of our own will, did transgress Thy commandment, and forsook Thy law, and sought to become gods like unto Thee, when Satan the enemy deceived us."

6 Then God said again unto Adam, "Because thou hast borne fear and trembling in this land, languor and suffering treading and walking about, going upon this mountain, and dying from it, I will take all this upon Myself in order to save thee."

CHAP. XXIII.

Adam and Eve gird themselves and make the first altar ever built.

THEN Adam wept more and said, "O God, have mercy on me, so far as to take upon Thee, that which I will do."

2 But God took His Word from Adam and Eve.

3 Then Adam and Eve stood on their feet; and Adam said to Eve "Gird thyself, and I also will gird myself." And she girded herself, as Adam told her.

4 Then Adam and Eve took stones and placed them in the shape of an altar; and they took leaves from the trees outside the garden, with which they wiped, from the face of the rock, the blood they had spilled.

5 But that which had dropped on the sand, they took together with the dust wherewith it was mingled and offered it upon the altar as an offering unto God.

6 Then Adam and Eve stood under the altar and wept, thus entreating God, "Forgive us our trespass [*1] and our sin, and look upon us with Thine eye of mercy. For when we were in the garden our praises and our hymns went up before Thee without ceasing.

7 "But when we came into this strange land, pure praise was no longer ours, nor righteous prayer, nor understanding hearts, nor sweet thoughts, nor just counsels, nor long discernment, nor upright feelings, neither is our bright nature left us. But our body is changed from the similitude in which it was at first, when we were created.

8 "Yet now look upon our blood which is offered upon these stones, and accept it at our hands, like the praise we used to sing unto Thee at first, when in the garden."

9 And Adam began to make more requests unto God.

Footnotes

^16:1 ORIGINAL OF THE LORD'S PRAYER SAID TO BE USED ABOUT 150 YEARS BEFORE OUR LORD: Our Father, Who art in Heaven, be gracious unto us, O Lord our God, hallowed be Thy Name, and let the remembrance of Thee be glorified in Heaven above and upon earth here below.

Let Thy kingdom reign over us now and forever. The Holy Men of old said remit and forgive unto all men whatsoever they have done unto me. And lead us not into temptation, but deliver us from the evil thing; for Thine is the kingdom and Thou shalt reign in glory forever and forevermore, AMEN.

CHAP. XXIV.

A vivid prophecy of the life and death of Christ.

TEN the merciful God, good 'and lover of men, looked upon Adam and Eve, and upon their blood, which they had held up as an offering unto Him; without an order from Him for so doing. But He wondered at them; and accepted their offerings.

2 And God sent from His presence a bright fire, that consumed their offering.

3 He smelt the sweet savour of their offering, and showed them mercy.

4 Then came the Word of God to Adam, and said unto him, "O Adam, as thou hast shed thy blood, so will I shed My own blood when I become flesh of thy seed; and as thou didst die, O Adam, so also will I die. And as thou didst build an

[36]

altar, so also will I make for thee an altar on the earth; and as thou didst offer thy blood upon it, so also will I offer My blood upon an altar on the earth.

5 "And as thou didst sue for forgiveness through that blood, so also will I make My blood forgiveness of sins, and blot out transgressions in it.

6 "And now, behold, I have accepted thy offering, O Adam, but the days of the covenant, wherein I have bound thee, are not fulfillled. When they are fulfillled, then will I bring thee back into the garden.

7 "Now, therefore, strengthen thy heart; and when sorrow comes upon thee, make Me an offering, and I will be favourable to thee."

CHAP. XXV.

God represented as merciful and loving. The establishing of worship.

BUT God knew that Adam had in his thoughts, that he should often kill himself and make an offering to Him of his blood.

2 Therefore did He say unto him, "O Adam, do not again kill thyself as thou didst, by throwing thyself down from that mountain."

3 But Adam said unto God, "It was in my mind to put an end to myself at once, for having transgressed Thy commandments, and for my having come out of the beautiful garden; and for the bright light of which Thou hast deprived me; and for the praises which poured forth from my mouth without ceasing, and for the light that covered me.

4 "Yet of Thy goodness, O God, do not away with me altogether; but be favourable to me every time I die, and bring me to life.

5 "And thereby it will be made known that Thou art a merciful God, who willest not that one should perish; who lovest not that one should fall; and who dost not condemn any one cruelly, badly, and by whole destruction."

6 Then Adam remained silent.

7 And the Word of God came unto him, and blessed him, and comforted him, and covenanted with him, that He would save him at the end of the days determined upon him.

8 This, then, was the first offering Adam made unto God; and so it became his custom to do.

CHAP. XXVI.

A beautiful prophecy of eternal life and joy (v. 15). The fall of night.

THEN Adam took Eve, and they began to return to the Cave of Treasures where they dwelt. But when they neared it and saw it from afar, heavy sorrow fell upon Adam and Eve when they looked at it.

2 Then Adam said to Eve, "When we were on the mountain we were comforted by the Word of God that conversed with us; and the light that came from the east, shone over us.

3 "But now the Word of God is hidden from us; and the light that shone over us is so changed as to disappear, and let darkness and sorrow come upon us.

4 "And we are forced to enter this cave which is like a prison, wherein darkness covers us, so that we are parted from each other; and thou canst not see me, neither can I see thee."

5 When Adam had said these words, they wept and spread their hands before God; for they were full of sorrow.

6 And they entreated God to bring the sun to them, to shine on them, so that darkness return not upon them, and they come not again under this covering of rock. And they wished to die rather than see the darkness.

7 Then God looked upon Adam and Eve and upon their great sorrow, and upon all they had done with a fervent heart, on account of all the trouble they were in, instead of their former well-being, and on account of all the misery that came upon them in a strange land.

8 Therefore God was not wroth with them; nor impatient with them; but He was longsuffering and forbearing towards them, as towards the children He had created.

9 Then came the Word of God to Adam, and said unto him, "Adam, as for the sun, if I were to take it and bring it to thee, days, hours, years and months would all come to naught, and the covenant I have made with thee, would never be fulfillled.

10 "But thou shouldest then be turned and left in a long plague, and no salvation would be left to thee for ever.

11 "Yea, rather, bear long and calm thy soul while thou abidest night and day; until the fulfillment of the days, and the time of My covenant is come.

12 "Then shall I come and save thee, O Adam, for I do not wish that thou be afflicted.

13 "And when I look at all the good things in which thou didst live, and why thou camest out of them, then would I willingly show thee mercy.

14 "But I cannot alter the covenant that has gone out of My mouth; else would I have brought thee back into the garden.

15 "When, however, the covenant is fulfillled, then shall I show thee and thy seed mercy, and bring thee into a land of gladness, where there is neither sorrow nor suffering; but abiding joy and gladness, and light that never fails, and praises that never cease; and a beautiful garden that shall never pass away."

16 And God said again unto Adam, "Be long-suffering and enter the cave, for the darkness, of which thou wast afraid, shall only be twelve hours long; and when ended, light shall arise."

17 Then when Adam heard these words from God, he and Eve worshipped before Him, and their hearts were comforted. They returned into the cave after their custom, while tears flowed from their eyes, sorrow and wailing came from their hearts, and they wished their soul would leave their body.

18 And Adam and Eve stood praying, until the darkness of night came upon them, and Adam was hid from Eve, and she from him.

19 And they remained standing in prayer.

CHAP. XXVII.

 The second tempting of Adam and Eve. The devil takes on the form of a beguiling light.

WHEN Satan, the hater of all good, saw how they continued in prayer, and how God communed with them, and comforted them, and how He had accepted their offering--Satan made an apparition.

2 He began with transforming his hosts; in his hands was a flashing fire, and they were in a great light.

3 He then placed his throne near the mouth of the cave because he could not enter into it by reason of their prayers. And he shed light into the cave, until the cave glistened over Adam and Eve; while his hosts began to sing praises.

4 And Satan did this, in order that when Adam saw the light, he should think within himself that it was a heavenly light, and that Satan's hosts were angels; and that God had sent them to watch at the cave, and to give him light in the darkness.

5 So that when Adam came out of the cave and saw them, and Adam and Eve bowed to Satan, then he would overcome Adam thereby, and a second time humble him before God.

6 When, therefore, Adam and Eve saw the light, fancying it was real, they strengthened their hearts; yet, as they were trembling, Adam said to Eve:--

7 "Look at that great light, and at those many songs of praise, and at that host standing outside that do not come in to us, do not tell us what they say, or whence they come, or what is the meaning of this light; what those praises are; wherefore they have been sent hither, and why they do not come in.

8 "If they were from God, they would come to us in the cave, and would tell us their errand."

9 Then Adam stood up and prayed unto God with a fervent heart, and said:--

10 "O Lord, is there in the world another god than Thou, who created angels and filled them with light, and sent them to keep us, who would come with them?

11 "But, lo, we see these hosts that stand at the mouth of the cave; they are in a great light; they sing loud praises. If they are of some other god than Thou, tell me; and if they are sent by Thee, inform me of the reason for which Thou hast sent them."

12 No sooner had Adam said this, than an angel from God appeared unto him in the cave, who said unto him, "O Adam, fear not. This is Satan and his hosts; he wishes to deceive you as he deceived you at first. For the first time, he was hidden in the serpent; but this time he is come to you in the similitude of an angel of light; in order that, when you worshipped him, he might enthrall you, in the very presence of God."

13 Then the angel went from Adam, and seized Satan at the opening of the cave, and stripped him of the feint he had assumed, and brought him in his own hideous form to Adam and Eve; who were afraid of him when they saw him.

14 And the angel said to Adam, "This hideous form has been his ever since God made him fall from heaven. He could not have come near you in it; therefore did he transform himself into an angel of light."

15 Then the angel drove away Satan and his hosts from Adam and Eve, and said unto them, "Fear not; God who created you, will strengthen you."

16 And the angel went from them.

17 But Adam and Eve remained standing in the cave; no consolation came to them; they were divided in their thoughts.

18 And when it was morning they prayed; and then went out to seek the garden. For their hearts were towards it, and they could get no consolation for having left it.

CHAP. XXVIII.

The Devil pretends to lead Adam and Eve to the water to bathe.

BUT when the wily Satan saw them, that they were going to the garden, he gathered together his host, and came in appearance upon a cloud, intent on deceiving them.

2 But when Adam and Eve saw him thus in a vision, they thought they were angels of God come to comfort them about their having left the garden, or to bring them back again into it.

3 And Adam spread his hands unto God, beseeching Him to make him understand what they were.

4 Then Satan, the hater of all good, said unto Adam, "O Adam, I am an angel of the great God; and, behold the hosts that surround me.

5 "God has sent me and them to take thee and bring thee to the border of the garden northwards; to the shore of the clear sea, and bathe thee and Eve in it, and raise you to your former gladness, that ye return again to the garden."

6 These words sank into the heart of Adam and Eve.

7 Yet God withheld His Word from Adam, and did not make him understand at once, but waited to see his strength; whether he would be overcome as Eve was when in the garden, or whether he would prevail.

8 Then Satan called to Adam and Eve, and said, "Behold, we go to the sea of water," and they began to go.

9 And Adam and Eve followed them at some little distance.

10 But when they came to the mountain to the north of the garden, a very high mountain, without any steps to the top of it, the Devil drew near to Adam and Eve, and made them go up to the top in reality, and not in a vision; wishing, as he did, to throw them down and kill them, and to wipe off their name from the earth; so that this earth should remain to him and his hosts alone.

CHAP. XXIX.

God tells Adam of the Devil's purpose. (v. 4).

BUT when the merciful God saw that Satan wished to kill Adam with his manifold devices, and saw that Adam was meek and without guile, God spake unto Satan in a loud voice, and cursed him.

2 Then he and his hosts fled, and Adam and Eve remained standing on the top of the mountain, whence they saw below them the wide world, high above which they were. But they saw none of the host which anon were by them.

3 They wept, both Adam and Eve, before God, and begged for forgiveness of Him.

4 Then came the Word from God to Adam, and said unto him, "Know thou and understand concerning this Satan, that he seeks to deceive thee and thy seed after thee."

5 And Adam wept before the Lord God, and begged and entreated Him to give him something from the garden, as a token to him, wherein to be comforted.

6 And God looked upon Adam's thought, and sent the angel Michael as far as the sea that reaches unto India, to take from thence golden rods and bring them to Adam.

7 This did God in His wisdom, in order that these golden rods, being with Adam in the cave, should shine forth with light in the night around him, and put an end to his fear of the darkness.

8 Then the angel Michael went down by God's order, took golden rods, as God had commanded him, and brought them to God.

CHAP. XXX.

Adam receives the first worldly goods.

AFTER these things, God commanded the angel Gabriel to go down to the garden, and say to the cherub who kept it, "Behold, God has commanded me to come into the garden, and to take thence sweet smelling incense, and give it to Adam."

2 Then the angel Gabriel went down by God's order to the garden, and told the cherub as God had commanded him.

3 The cherub then said, "Well." And Gabriel went in and took the incense.

4 Then God commanded His angel Raphael to go down to the garden, and speak to the cherub about some myrrh, to give to Adam.

5 And the angel Raphael went down and told the cherub as God had commanded him, and the cherub said, "Well." Then Raphael went in and took the myrrh.

6 The golden rods were from the Indian sea, where there are precious stones. The incense was from the eastern border of the garden; and the myrrh from the western border, whence bitterness came upon Adam.

7 And the angels brought these three things to God, by the Tree of Life, in the garden.

8 Then God said to the angels, "Dip them in the spring of water; then take them and sprinkle their water over Adam and Eve, that they be a little comforted in their sorrow, and give them to Adam and Eve.

9 And the angels did as God had commanded them, and they gave all those things to Adam and Eve on the top of the mountain upon which Satan had placed them, when he sought to make an end of them.

10 And when Adam saw the golden rods, the incense and the myrrh, he was rejoiced and wept because he thought that the gold was a token of the kingdom whence he had come, that the incense was a token of the bright light which had been taken from him, and that the myrrh was a token of the sorrow in which he was.

CHAP. XXXI.

 They make themselves more comfortable in the Cave of Treasures on the third day.

AFTER thcsc things God said unto Adam, "Thou didst ask of Me something from the garden, to be comforted therewith, and I have given thee these three tokens as a consolation to thee; that thou trust in Me and in My covenant with thee.

2 "For I will come and save thee; and kings shall bring me when in the flesh, gold, incense and myrrh; gold as a token of My kingdom; incense as a token of My divinity; and myrrh as a token of My suffering and of My death.

3 "But, O Adam, put these by thee in the cave; the gold that it may shed light over thee by night; the incense, that thou smell its sweet savour; and the myrrh, to comfort thee in thy sorrow."

4 When Adam heard these words from God, he worshipped before Him. He and Eve worshipped Him and gave Him thanks, because He had dealt mercifully with them.

5 Then God commanded the three angels, Michael, Gabriel and Raphael, each to bring what he had brought, and give it to Adam. And they did so, one by one.

6 And God commanded Suriyel and Salathiel to bear up Adam and Eve, and bring them down from the top of the high mountain, and to take them to the Cave of Treasures.

7 There they laid the gold on the south side of the cave, the incense on the eastern side, and the myrrh on the western side. For the mouth of the cave was on the north side.

8 The angels then comforted Adam and Eve, and departed.

9 The gold was seventy rods; the incense, twelve pounds; and the myrrh, three pounds.

10 These remained by Adam in the House of Treasures; therefore was it called "of concealment." But other interpreters say it was called the "Cave of Treasures," by reason of the bodies of righteous men that were in it.

11 These three things did God give to Adam, on the third day after he had come out of the garden, in token of the three days the Lord should remain in the heart of the earth.

12 And these three things, as they continued with Adam in the cave, gave him light by night; and by day they gave him a little relief from his sorrow.

CHAP. XXXII.

Adam and Eve go into the water to pray.

AND Adam and Eve remained in the Cave of Treasures until the seventh day; they neither ate of the fruit of the earth, nor drank water.

2 And when it dawned on the eighth day, Adam said to Eve, "O Eve, we prayed God to give us somewhat from the garden, and He sent His angels who brought us what we had desired.

3 "But now, arise, let us go to the sea of water we saw at first, and let us stand in it, praying that God will again be favourable to us and take us back to the garden; or give us something; or that He will give us comfort in some other land than this in which we are."

4 Then Adam and Eve came out of the cave, went and stood on the border of the sea in which they had before thrown themselves, and Adam said to Eve:--

5 "Come, go down into this place, and come not out of it until the end of thirty days, when I shall come to thee. And pray to God with fervent heart and a sweet voice, to forgive us.

6 "And I will go to another place, and go down into it, and do like thee."

7 Then Eve went down into the water, as Adam had commanded her. Adam also went down into the water; and they stood praying; and besought the Lord to forgive them their offence, and to restore them to their former state.

8 And they stood thus praying, unto the end of the five-and-thirty days.

CHAP. XXXIII.

Satan falsely promises the "bright light!'

BUT Satan, the hater of all good, sought them in the cave, but found them not, although he searched diligently for them.

2 But he found them standing in the water praying and thought within himself, "Adam and Eve are thus standing in that water beseeching God to forgive them their transgression, and to restore them to their former estate, and to take them from under my hand.

3 "But I will deceive them so that they shall come out of the water, and not fulfill their vow."

4 Then the hater of all good, went not to Adam, but be went to Eve, and took the form of an angel of God, praising and rejoicing, and said to her--

5 "Peace be unto thee! Be glad and rejoice! God is favourable unto you, and He sent me to Adam. I have brought him the glad tidings of salvation, and of his being filled with bright light as he was at first.

6 "And Adam, in his joy for his restoration, has sent me to thee, that thou come to me, in order that I crown thee with light like him.

7 "And he said to me, 'Speak unto Eve; if she does not come with thee, tell her of the sign when we were on the top of the mountain; how God sent His angels who took us and brought us to the Cave of Treasures; and laid the gold on the southern side; incense, on the eastern side; and myrrh on the western side.' Now come to him."

8 When Eve heard these words from him, she rejoiced greatly. And thinking that Satan's appearance was real, she came out of the sea.

9 He went before, and she followed him until they came to Adam. Then Satan hid himself from her, and she saw him no more.

10 She then came and stood before Adam, who was standing by the water and rejoicing in God's forgiveness.

11 And as she called to him, he turned round, found her there and wept when he saw her, and smote upon his breast; and from the bitterness of his grief, he sank into the water.

12 But God looked upon him and upon his misery, and upon his being about to breathe his last. And the Word of God came from heaven, raised him out of the water, and said unto him, "Go up the high bank to Eve." And when he came up to Eve he said unto her, "Who said to thee 'come hither'?"

13 Then she told him the discourse of the angel who had appeared unto her and had given her a sign.

14 But Adam grieved, and gave her to know it was Satan. He then took her and they both returned to the cave.

15 These things happened to them the second time they went down to the water, seven days after their coming out of the garden.

16 They fasted in the water thirty-five days; altogether forty-two days since they had left the garden.

CHAP. XXXIV.

 Adam recalls the creation of Eve. He eloquently appeals for food and drink.

AND on the morning of the forty-third day, they came out of the cave, sorrowful and weeping. Their bodies were lean, and they were parched from hunger and thirst, from fasting and praying, and from their heavy sorrow on account of their transgression.

2 And when they had come out of the cave they went up the mountain to the west of the garden.

3 There they stood and prayed and besought God to grant them forgiveness of their sins.

4 And after their prayers Adam began to entreat 'God, saying, "O my Lord my God, and my Creator, thou didst command the four elements to be gathered together, and they were gathered together by Thine order.

5 "Then Thou spreadest Thy hand and didst create me out of one element, that of dust of the earth; and Thou didst bring me into the garden at the third hour, on a Friday, and didst inform me of it in the cave.

6 "Then, at first, I knew neither night nor day, for I had a bright nature; neither did the light in which I lived ever leave me to know night or day.

7 "Then, again, O Lord, in that third hour in which Thou didst create me, Thou broughtest to me all beasts, and lions, and ostriches, and fowls of the air, and all things that move in the earth, which Thou hadst created at the first hour before me of the Friday.

8 "And Thy will was that I should name them all, one by one, with a suitable name. But Thou gavest me understanding and knowledge, and a pure heart and a right mind from Thee, that I should name them after Thine own mind regarding the naming of them.

9 "O God, Thou madest them obedient to me, and didst order that not one of them break from my sway, according to Thy commandment, and to the dominion which Thou hast given me over them. But now they are all estranged from me.

10 "Then it was in that third hour of Friday, in which Thou didst create me, and didst command me concerning the tree, to which I was neither to draw near, nor to eat thereof; for Thou saidst to me in the garden, 'When thou eatest of it, of death thou shalt die.'

11 "And if Thou hadst punished me as Thou saidst, with death, I should have died that very moment.

12 "Moreover, when Thou commandedst me regarding the tree, I was neither to approach nor to eat thereof, Eve was not with me; Thou hadst not Yet created her, neither hadst Thou yet taken her out of my side; nor had she yet heard this order from Thee.

13 "Then, at the end of the third hour of that Friday, O Lord, Thou didst cause a slumber and a sleep to come over me, and I slept, and was overwhelmed in sleep.

14 "Then Thou didst draw a rib out of my side, and created it after my own similitude and image. Then I awoke; and when I saw her and knew who she was, I said, 'This is bone of my bones, and flesh of my flesh; henceforth she shall be called woman.'

15 "It was of Thy good will, O God, that Thou broughtest a slumber and a sleep over me, and that Thou didst forthwith bring Eve out of my side, until she was out, so that I did not see how she was made; neither could I witness, O my Lord, how awful and great are Thy goodness and glory.

16 "And of Thy goodwill, O Lord, Thou madest us both with bodies of a bright nature, and Thou madest us two, one; and Thou gavest us Thy grace, and didst fill us with praises of the Holy Spirit; that we should be neither hungry nor thirsty, nor know what sorrow is, nor yet faintness of heart; neither suffering, fasting, nor weariness.

17 "But now, O God, since we transgressed Thy commandment and broke Thy law, Thou hast brought us out into a strange land, and has caused suffering, and faintness, hunger and thirst to come upon us.

1S "Now, therefore, O God, we pray Thee, give us something to eat from the garden, to satisfy our hunger with it; and something wherewith to quench our thirst.

19 "For, behold, many days, O God, we have tasted nothing and drunk nothing, and our flesh is dried up, and our strength is wasted, and sleep is gone from our eyes from faintness and weeping.

20 "Then, O God, we dare not gather aught of the fruit of trees, from fear of Thee. For when we transgressed at first Thou didst spare us, and didst not make us die.

21 "But now, we thought in our hearts, if we eat of the fruit of trees, without God's order, He will destroy us this time, and will wipe us off from the face of the earth.

22 "And if we drink of this water, without God's order, He will make an end of us, and root us up at once.

23 "Now, therefore, O God, that I am come to this place with Eve, we beg Thou wilt give us of the fruit of the garden, that we may be satisfied with it.

24 "For we desire the fruit that is on the earth, and all else that we lack in it."

CHAP. XXXV.

God's reply.

THEN God looked again upon Adam and his weeping and groaning, and the Word of God came to him, and said unto him:--

2 "O Adam, when thou wast in My garden, thou knewest neither eating nor drinking; neither faintness nor suffering; neither leanness of flesh, nor change; neither did sleep depart from thine eyes. But since thou transgressedst, and camest into this strange land, all these trials are come upon thee."

CHAP. XXXVI.

Figs.

THEN God commanded the cherub, who kept the gate of the garden with a sword of fire in his hand, to take some of the fruit of the fig-tree, and to give it to Adam.

2 The cherub obeyed the command of the Lord God, and went into the garden and brought two figs on two twigs, each fig hanging to its leaf; they were from two of the trees among which Adam and Eve hid themselves when God went to walk in the garden, and the Word of God came to Adam and Eve and said unto them, "Adam, Adam, where art thou?"

3 And Adam answered, "O God, here am I. When I heard the sound of Thee and Thy voice, I hid myself, because I am naked."

4 Then the cherub took two figs and brought them to Adam and Eve. But he threw them to them from afar; for they might not come near the cherub by reason of their flesh, that could not come near the fire.

5 At first, angels trembled at the presence of Adam and were afraid of him. But now Adam trembled before the angels and was afraid of them.

6 Then Adam drew near and took one fig, and Eve also came in turn and took the other.

7 And as they took them up in their hands, they looked at them, and knew they were from the trees among which they had hidden them elves.

CHAP. XXXVII.

Forty-three days of penance do not redeem one hour of sin (v. 6).

THEN Adam said to Eve, "Seest thou not these figs and their leaves, with which we covered ourselves when we were stripped of our bright nature? But now, we know not what misery and suffering may come upon us from eating them.

2 "Now, therefore, O Eve, let us restrain ourselves and not eat of them, thou and I; and let us ask God to give us of the fruit of the Tree of Life."

3 Thus did Adam and Eve restrain themselves, and did not eat of these figs.

4 But Adam began to pray to God and to beseech Him to give him of the fruit of the Tree of Life, saying thus: "O God, when we transgressed Thy commandment

at the sixth hour of Friday, we were stripped of the bright nature we had, and did not continue in the garden after our transgression, more than three hours.

5 "But on the evening Thou madest us come out of it. O God, we transgressed against Thee one hour, and all these trials and sorrows have come upon us until this day.

6 "And those days together with this the forty-third day, do not redeem that one hour in which we transgressed!

7 "O God, look upon us with an eye of pity, and do not requite us according to our transgression of Thy commandment, in presence of Thee.

8 "O, God, give us of the fruit of the Tree of Life, that we may eat of it, and live, and turn not to see sufferings and other trouble, in this earth; for Thou art God.

9 "When we transgressed Thy commandment, Thou madest us come out of the garden, and didst send a cherub to keep the Tree of Life, lest we should eat thereof, and live; and know nothing of faintness after we transgressed.

10 "But now, O Lord, behold, we have endured all these days, and have borne sufferings. Make these forty-three days an equivalent for the one hour in which we transgressed."

CHAP. XXXVIII.

"When 5500 years are fulfilled . . . ."

AFTER these things the Word of God came to Adam, and said unto him:--

2 "O Adam, as to the fruit of the Tree of Life, for which thou askest, I will not give it thee now, but when the 5500 years are fulfilled. Then will I give thee of the fruit of the Tree of Life, and thou shalt eat, and live for ever, thou, and Eve, and thy righteous seed.

3 "But these forty-three days cannot make amends for the hour in which thou didst transgress My commandment.

4 "O Adam, I gave thee to eat of the fig-tree in which thou didst hide thyself. Go and eat of it, thou and Eve.

5 "I will not deny thy request, neither will I disappoint thy hope; therefore, bear up unto the fulfillment of the covenant I made with thee."

6 And God withdrew His Word from Adam.

CHAP. XXXIX.

Adam is cautious--but too late.

THEN Adam returned to Eve, and said to her, "Arise, and take a fig for thyself, and I will take another; and let us go to our cave."

2 Then Adam and Eve took each a fig and went towards the cave; the time was about the setting of the sun; and their thoughts made them long to eat of the fruit.

3 But Adam said to Eve, "I am afraid to eat of this fig. I know not what may come upon me from it."

4 So Adam wept, and stood praying before God, saying, "Satisfy my hunger, without my having to eat this fig; for after I have eaten it, what will it profit me? And what shall I desire and ask of Thee, O God, when it is gone?"

5 And he said again, "I am afraid to eat of it; for I know not what will befall me through it."

CHAP. XL.

The first Human hunger.

THEN the Word of God came to Adam, and said unto him, "O, Adam, why hadst thou not this dread, neither this fasting, nor this care ere this? And why hadst thou not this fear before thou didst transgress?

2 "But when thou camest to dwell in this strange land, thy animal body could not be on earth without earthly food, to strengthen it and to restore its powers."

3 And God withdrew His Word from Adam.

[54]

CHAP. XLI.

The first Human thirst.

THEN Adam took the fig, and laid it on the golden rods. Eve also took her fig, and put it upon the incense.

2 And the weight of each fig was that of a water-melon; for the fruit of the garden was much larger than the fruit of this land.

3 But Adam and Eve remained standing and fasting the whole of that night, until the morning dawned.

4 When the sun rose they were at their prayers, and Adam said to Eve, after they had done praying:--

5 "O Eve, come, let us go to the border of the garden looking south; to the place whence the river flows, and is parted into four heads. There we will pray to God, and ask Him to give us to drink of the Water of Life.

6 "For God has not fed us with the Tree of Life, in order that we may not live. We will, therefore, ask him to give us of the Water of Life, and to quench our thirst with it, rather than with a drink of water of this land."

7 When Eve heard these words from Adam, she agreed; and they both arose and came to the southern border of the garden, upon the brink of the river of water at some little distance from the garden.

8 And they stood and prayed before the Lord, and asked Him to look upon them this once, to forgive them, and to grant them their request.

9 After this prayer from both of them, Adam began to pray with his voice before God, and said:--

10 "O Lord, when I was in the garden and saw the water that flowed from under the Tree of Life, my heart did not desire, neither did my body require to drink of it; neither did I know thirst, for I was living; and above that which I am now.

11 "So that in order to live I did not require any Food of Life, neither did I drink of the Water of Life.

12 "But now, O God, I am dead; my flesh is parched with thirst. Give me of the Water of Life that I may drink of it and live.

13 "Of Thy mercy, O God, save me from these plagues and trials, and bring me into another land different from this, if Thou wilt not let me dwell in Thy garden."

CHAP. XLII.

 A promise of the Water of Life. The third prophecy of the coming of Christ.

THEN came the Word of God to Adam, and said unto him:--

2 "O Adam, as to what thou sayest, 'Bring me into a land where there is rest,' it is not another land than this, but it is the kingdom of heaven where alone there is rest.

3 "But thou canst not make thy entrance into it at present; but only after thy judgment is past and fulfillled.

4 "Then will I make thee go up into the kingdom of heaven, thee and thy righteous seed; and I will give thee and them the rest thou askest for at present.

5 "And if thou saidst, 'Give me of the Water of Life that I may drink and live'--it cannot be this day, but on the day that I shall descend into hell, and break the gates of brass, and bruise in pieces the kingdoms of iron.

6 "Then will I in mercy save thy soul and the souls of the righteous, to give them rest in My garden. And that shall be when the end of the world is come.

7 "And, again, as regards the Water of Life thou seekest, it will not be granted thee this day; but on the day that I shall shed My blood upon thy head in the land of Golgotha.

8 "For My blood shall be the Water of Life unto thee, at that time, and not to thee alone, but unto all those of thy seed who shall believe in Me; that it be unto them for rest for ever."

9 The Lord said again unto Adam, "O Adam, when thou wast in the garden, these trials did not come to thee

10 "But since thou didst transgress My commandment, all these sufferings have come upon thee.

11. "Now, also, does thy flesh require food and drink; drink then of that water that flows by thee on the face of the earth."

12 Then God withdrew His Word from Adam.

13 And Adam and Eve worshipped the Lord, and returned from the river of water to the cave. It was noon-day; and when they drew near to the cave, they saw a large fire by it.

CHAP. XLIII.

 The Devil attempts arson.

THEN Adam and Eve were afraid, and stood still. And Adam said to Eve, "What is that fire by our cave? We do nothing in it to bring about this fire.

2 "We neither have bread to bake therein, nor broth to cook there. As to this fire, we know not the like, neither do we know what to call it.

3 "But ever since God sent the cherub with a sword of fire that flashed and lightened in his hand, from fear of which we fell down and were like corpses, have we not seen the like.

4 "But now O Eve, behold, this is the same fire that was in the cherub's hand, which God has sent to keep the cave in which we dwell.

5 "O Eve, it is because God is angry with us, and will drive us from it.

6 "O Eve, we have again transgressed His commandment in that cave, so that He had sent this fire to burn around it, and to prevent us from going into it.

7 "If this be really so, O Eve, where shall we dwell? And whither shall we flee from before the face of the Lord? Since, as regards the garden, He will not let us abide in it, and He has deprived us of the good things thereof; but He has placed

us in this cave, in which we have borne darkness, trials and hardships, until at last we found comfort therein.

8 "But now that He has brought us out into another land, who knows what may happen in it? And who knows but that the darkness of that land may be far greater than the darkness of this land?

9 "Who knows what may happen in that land by day or by night? And who knows whether it will be far or near, O Eve? Where it will please God to put us, may be far from the garden, O Eve! or where God will prevent us from beholding Him, because we have transgressed His commandment, and because we have made requests unto Him at all times?

10 "O Eve, if God will bring us into a strange land other than this, in which we find consolation, it must be to put our souls to death, and blot out our name from the face of the earth.

11 "O Eve, if we are farther estranged from the garden and from God, where shall we find Him again, and ask Him to give us gold, incense, myrrh, and some fruit of the fig-tree?

12 "Where shall we find Him, to comfort us a second time? Where shall we find Him, that He may think of us, as regards the covenant He has made on our behalf T'

13 Then Adam said no more. And they kept looking, he and Eve, towards the cave, and at the fire that flared up around it.

14 But that fire was from Satan. For he had gathered trees and dry grasses, and had carried and brought them to the cave, and had set fire to them, in order to consume the cave and--what was in it.

15 So that Adam and Eve should be left in sorrow, and he should cut off their trust in God, and make them deny Him.

16 But by the mercy of God he could not burn the cave, for God sent His angel round the cave to guard it from such a fire, until it went out.

17 And this fire lasted from noon-day until the break of day. That was the forty-fifth day.

[58]

CHAP. XLIV.

The power of fire over man.

YET Adam and Eve were standing and looking at the fire, and unable to come near the cave from their dread of the fire.

2 And Satan kept on bringing trees and throwing them into the fire, until the flame thereof rose up on high, and covered the whole cave, thinking, as he did in his own mind, to consume the cave with much fire. But the angel of the Lord was guarding it.

3 And yet he could not curse Satan, nor injure him by word, because he had no authority over him, neither did he take to doing so with words from his mouth.

4 Therefore did the angel bear with him, without saying one bad word until the Word of God came who said to Satan, "Go hence; once before didst thou deceive My servants, and this time thou seekest to destroy them.

5 "Were it not for My mercy I would have destroyed thee and thy hosts from off the earth. But I have had patience with thee, unto the end of the world."

6 Then Satan fled from before the Lord. But the fire went on burning around the cave like a coal-fire the whole day; which was the forty-sixth day Adam and Eve had spent since they came out of the garden.

7 And when Adam and Eve saw that the heat of the fire had somewhat cooled down, they began to walk towards the cave to get into it as they were wont; but they could not, by reason of the heat of the fire.

8 Then they both took to weeping because of the fire that made separation between them and the cave, and that drew towards them, burning. And they were afraid.

9 Then Adam said to Eve, "See this fire of which we have a portion in us: which formerly yielded to us, but no longer does so, now that we have transgressed the limit of creation, and changed our condition, and our nature is altered. But the fire is not changed in its nature, nor altered from its creation. Therefore has it now power over us; and when we come near it, it scorches our flesh."

[59]

CHAP. XLV.

Why Satan didn't fulfill his promises.

THEN Adam rose and prayed unto God, saying, "See, this fire has made separation between us and the cave in which Thou hast commanded us to dwell; but now, behold, we cannot go into it."

2 Then God heard Adam, and sent him His Word, that said:--

3 "O Adam, see this fire! how different the flame and heat thereof are from the garden of delights and the good things in it!

4 "When thou wast under My control, all creatures yielded to thee; but after thou hast transgressed My commandment, they all rise over thee."

5 Again said God unto him, "See, O Adam, how Satan has exalted thee! He has deprived thee of the Godhead, and of an exalted state like unto Me, and has not kept his word to thee; but, after all, is become thy foe. It is he who made this fire in which he meant to burn thee and Eve.

6 "Why, O Adam, has he not kept his agreement with thee, not even one day; but has deprived thee of the glory that was on thee--when thou didst yield to his command?

7 "Thinkest thou, Adam, that he loved thee when he made this agreement with thee? Or, that he loved thee and wished to raise thee on high?

8 "But no, Adam, he did not do all that out of love to thee; but he wished to make thee come out of light into darkness, and from an exalted state to degradation; from glory to abasement; from joy to sorrow; and from rest to fasting and fainting."

9 God said also to Adam, "See this fire kindled by Satan around thy cave; see this wonder that surrounds thee; and know that it will encompass about both thee and thy seed, when ye hearken to his behest; that he will plague you with fire; and that ye shall go down into hell after ye are dead.

10 "Then shall ye see the burning of his fire, that will thus be burning around you and your seed. There shall be no deliverance from it for you, but at My coming; in

like manner as thou canst not now go into thy cave, by reason of the great fire around it; not until My Word shall come that will make a way for thee on the day My covenant is fulfillled.

11 "There is no way for thee at present to come from hence to rest, not until My Word comes, who is My Word. Then will He make a way for thee, and thou shalt have rest." Then God called with His Word to that fire that burned around the cave, that it part itself asunder, until Adam had gone through it. Then the fire parted itself by God's order, and a way was made for Adam.

12 And God withdrew His Word from Adam.

CHAP. XLVI.

"How many times have I delivered thee out of his hand . . ."

THEN Adam and Eve began again to come into the cave. And when they came to the way between the fire, Satan blew into the fire like a whirlwind, and made on Adam and Eve a burning coal-fire; so that their bodies were singed; and the coal-fire scorched them.

2 And from the burning of the fire Adam and Eve cried aloud, and said, "O Lord, save us! Leave us not to be consumed and plagued by this burning fire; neither require us for having transgressed Thy commandment."

3 Then God looked upon their bodies, on which Satan had caused fire to bum, and God sent His angel that stayed the burning fire. But the wounds remained on their bodies.

4 And God said unto Adam, "See Satan's love for thee, who pretended to give thee the Godhead and greatness; and, behold, he burns thee with fire, and seeks to destroy thee from off the earth.

5 "Then look at Me, O Adam; I created thee, and how many times have I delivered thee out of his hand? If not, would he not have destroyed thee?"

6 God said again to Eve, "What is that he promised thee in the garden, saying, 'At the time ye shall eat of the tree, your eyes will be opened, and you shall become like gods, knowing good and evil.' But lo! he has burnt your bodies with fire, and

has made you taste the taste of fire, for the taste of the garden; and has made you see the burning of fire, and the evil thereof, and the power it has over you.

7 "Your eyes have seen the good he has taken from you, and in truth he has opened your eyes; and you have seen the garden in which ye were with Me, and ye have also seen the evil that has come upon you from Satan. But as to the Godhead he cannot give it you, neither fulfill his speech to you. Nay, he was bitter against you and your seed, that will come after you."

8 And God withdrew His Word from them.

CHAP. XLVII.

The Devil's own Scheming.

THEN Adam and Eve came into the cave, yet trembling at the fire that had scorched their bodies. So Adam said to Eve:--

2 "Lo, the fire has burnt our flesh in this world; but how will it be when we are dead, and Satan shall punish our souls? Is not our deliverance long and far off, unless God come, and in mercy to us fulfill His promise?"

3 Then Adam and Eve passed into the cave, blessing themselves for coming into it once more. For it was in their thoughts, that they never should enter it, when they saw the fire around it.

4 But as the sun was setting the fire was still burning and nearing Adam and Eve in the cave, so that they could not sleep in it. After the sun had set, they went out of it. This was the forty-seventh day after they came out of the garden.

5 Adam and Eve then came under the top of hill by the garden to sleep, as they were wont.

6 And they stood and prayed God to forgive them their sins, and then fell asleep under the summit of the mountain.

7 But Satan, the hater of all good, thought within himself: Whereas God has promised salvation to Adam by covenant, and that He would deliver him out of all the hardships that have befallen him-but has not promised me by covenant, and will not deliver me out of my hardships; nay, since He has promised him that He

should make him and his seed dwell in the kingdom in which I once was--I will kill Adam.

8 The earth shall be rid of him; and shall be left to me alone; so that when he is dead
he may not have any seed left to inherit the kingdom that shall remain my own realm; God will then be in want of me, and He will restore me to it with my hosts.

CHAP XLVIII.

Fifth apparition of Satan to Adam and Eve.

AFTER this Satan called to his hosts, all of which came to him, and said unto him:--

2 "O, our Lord, what wilt thou do?"

3 He then said unto them, "Ye know that this Adam, whom God created out of the dust, is he who has taken our kingdom. Come, let us gather together and kill him; or hurl a rock at him and at Eve, and crush them under it."

4 When Satan's hosts heard these words, they came to the part of the mountain where Adam and Eve were asleep.

5 Then Satan and his hosts took a huge rock, broad and even, and without blemish, thinking within himself, "If there should be a hole in the rock, when it fell on them, the hole in the rock might come upon them, and so they would escape and not die."

6 He then said to his hosts, "Take up this stone, and throw it flat upon them, so that it roll not from them to somewhere else. And when ye have hurled it, flee and tarry not."

7 And they did as he bid them. But as the rock fell down from the mountain upon Adam and Eve, God commanded it to become a kind of shed over them, that did them no harm. And so it was by God's order.

8 But when the rock fell, the whole earth quaked with it, and. was shaken from the size of the rock.

9 And as it quaked and shook, Adam and Eve awoke from sleep, and found themselves under a rock like a shed. But they knew not how it was; for when they fell asleep they were under the sky, and not under a shed; and when they saw it, they were afraid.

10 Then Adam said to Eve, "Wherefore has the mountain bent itself, and the earth quaked and shaken on our account? And why has this rock spread itself over us like a tent?

11 "Does God intend to plague us and to shut us up in this prison? Or will He close the earth upon us?

12 "He is angry with us for our having come out of the cave without His order; and for our having done so of our own accord, without consulting Him, when we left the cave and came to this place."

13 Then Eve said, "If, indeed, the earth quaked for our sake, and this rock forms a tent over us because of our transgression, then woe be to us, O Adam, for our punishment will be long.

14 "But arise and pray Ito God to let us know concerning this, and what this rock is, that is spread over us like a tent."

15 Then Adam stood up and prayed before the Lord, to let him know about this strait. And Adam thus stood praying until the morning.

CHAP. XLIX.

The first prophecy of the Resurrection.

THEN the Word of God came and said:--

2 "O Adam, who counselled thee, when thou earnest out of the cave, to come to this place?"

3 And Adam said unto God, "O Lord, we came to this place because of the heat of the fire, that came upon us inside the cave."

4 Then the Lord God said unto Adam, "O Adam, thou dreadest the heat of fire for one night, but how will it be when thou dwellest in hell?

5 "Yet, O Adam, fear not, neither say in thy heart that I have spread this rock as an awning over thee, to plague thee therewith.

6 "It came from Satan, who had promised thee the Godhead and majesty. It is he who threw down this rock to kill thee under it, and Eve with thee, and thus to prevent you from living upon the earth.

7 "But, in mercy for you, just as that rock was falling down upon you, I commanded it to form an awning over you; and the rock under you, to lower itself.

8 "And this sign, O Adam, will happen to Me at My coming upon earth: Satan will raise the people of the Jews Jo put Me to death; and they will lay Me in a rock, and seal a large stone upon Me, and I shall remain within that rock three days and three nights.

9 "But on the third day I shall rise again, and it shall be salvation to thee, O Adam, and to thy seed, to believe in Me. But, O Adam, I will not bring thee from under this rock until three days and three nights are passed."

10 And God withdrew His Word from Adam.

11 But Adam and Eve abode under the rock three days and three nights, as God had told them.

12 And God did so to them because they had left their cave and had come to this same place without God's order.

13 But, after three days and three nights, God opened the rock and brought them out from under it. Their flesh was dried up, and their eyes and their hearts were troubled from weeping and sorrow.

CHAP. L.

Adam and Eve seek to cover their nakedness.

THEN Adam and Eve went forth and came into the Cave of Treasures, and they stood praying in it the whole of that day, until the evening.

2 And this took place at the end of fifty days after they had left the garden.

3 But Adam and Eve rose again and prayed to God in the cave the whole of that night, and begged for mercy from Him.

4 And when the day dawned, Adam said unto Eve, "Come! let us go and do some work for our bodies."

5 So they went out of the cave, and came to the northern border of the garden, and they sought something to cover their bodies withal. But they found nothing, and knew not how to do the work. Yet their bodies were stained, and they were speechless from cold and heat.

6 Then Adam stood and asked God to show him something wherewith to cover their bodies.

7 Then came the Word of God and said unto him, "O Adam, take Eve and come to the seashore, where ye fasted before. There ye shall find skins of sheep, whose flesh was devoured by lions, and whose skins were left. Take them and make raiment for yourselves, and clothe yourselves withal."

CHAP. LI.

"What is his beauty that you should have followed him?"

WHEN Adam heard these words from God, he took Eve and removed from the northern end of the garden to the south of it, by the river of water, where they once fasted.

2 But as they were going in the way, and before they reached that place, Satan, the wicked one, had heard the Word of God communing with Adam respecting his covering.

3 It grieved him, and he hastened to the place where the sheep-skins were, with the intention of taking them and throwing them into the sea, or of burning them with fire, that Adam and Eve should not find them.

4 But as he was about to take them, the Word of God came from heaven, and bound him by the side of those skins until Adam and Eve came near him. But as they neared him they were afraid of him, and of his hideous look.

5 Then came the Word of God to Adam and Eve, and said to them, "This is he who was hidden in the serpent, and who deceived you, and stripped you of the garment of light and glory in which you were.

6 "This is he who promised you majesty and divinity. Where, then, is the beauty that was on him? Where is his divinity? Where is his light? Where is the glory that rested on him?

7 "Now his figure is hideous; he is become abominable among angels; and he has come to be called Satan.

8 "O Adam I he wished to take from you this earthly garment of sheep-skins, and to destroy it, and not let you be covered with it.

9 "What, then, is his beauty that you should have followed him? And what have you gained by hearkening to him? See his evil works and then look at Me; at Me, your Creator, and at the good deeds I do you.

10 "See, I bound him until you came and saw him and beheld his weakness, that no power is left with him."

11 And God released him from his bonds.

CHAP. LII.

Adam and Eve sew the first shirt.

AFTER this Adam and Eve said no more, but wept before God on account of their creation, and of their bodies that required an earthly covering.

2 Then Adam said unto Eve, "O Eve, this is the skin of beasts with which we shall be covered. But when we have put it on, behold, a token of death shall have come upon us, inasmuch as the owners of these skins have died, and have wasted away. So also shall we die, and pass away."

3 Then Adam and Eve took the skins, and went back to the Cave of Treasures; and when in it, they stood and prayed as they were wont.

4 And they thought how they could make garments of those skins; for they had no skill for it.

5 Then God sent to them His angel to show them how to work it out. And the angel said to Adam, "Go forth, and bring some palm-thorns." Then Adam went out, and brought some, as the angel had commanded him.

6 Then the angel began before them to work out the skins, after the manner of one who prepares a shirt. And he took the thorns and stuck them into the skins, before their eyes.

7 Then the angel again stood up and prayed God that the thorns in those skins should be hidden, so as to be, as it were, sewn with one thread.

8 And so it was, by God's order; they became garments for Adam and Eve, and He clothed them withal.

9 From that time the nakedness of their bodies was covered from the sight of each other's eyes.

10 And this happened at the end of the fifty-first day.

11 Then when Adam's and Eve's bodies were covered, they stood and prayed, and sought mercy of the Lord, and forgiveness, and gave Him thanks for that He had had mercy on them, and had covered their nakedness. And they ceased not from prayer the whole of that night.

12 Then when the mom dawned at the rising of the sun, they said their prayers after their custom; and then went out of the cave.

13 And Adam said unto Eve, "Since we know not what there is to the westward of this cave, let us go forth and see it to-day." Then they came forth and went towards the western border.

CHAP. LIII.

The prophecy of the Western Lands.

THEY were not very far from the cave, when Satan came towards them, and hid himself between them and the cave, under the form of two ravenous lions three days without food, that came towards Adam and Eve, as if to break them in pieces and devour them.

2 Then Adam and Eve wept, and prayed God to deliver them from their paws.

3 Then the Word of God came to them, and drove away the lions from them.

4 And God said unto Adam, "O Adam, what seekest thou on the western border? And why hast thou left of thine own accord the eastern border, in which was thy dwelling-place?

5 "Now, then, turn back to thy cave, and remain in it, that Satan do not deceive thee, nor work his purpose upon thee.

6 "For in this western border, O Adam, there will go from thee a seed, that shall replenish it; and that will defile themselves with their sins, and with their yielding to the behests of Satan, and by following his works.

7 "Therefore will I bring upon them the waters of a flood, and overwhelm them all. But I will deliver what is left of the righteous among them; and I will bring them to a distant land, and the land in which thou dwellest now shall remain desolate and without one inhabitant in it."

8 After God had thus discoursed to them, they went back to the Cave of Treasures. But their flesh was dried up, and their strength failed from fasting and praying, and from the sorrow they felt at having trespassed against God.

CHAP. LIV.

Adam and Eve go exploring.

THEN Adam and Eve stood up in the cave and prayed the whole of that night until the morning dawned. And when the sun was risen they both went out of the cave; their heads wandering from heaviness of sorrow, and they not knowing whither they went.

2 And they walked thus unto the southern border of the garden. And they began to go up that border until they came to the eastern border beyond which there was no farther space.

3 And the cherub who guarded the garden was standing at the western gate, and guarding it against Adam and Eve, lest they should suddenly come into the garden. And the cherub turned round, as if to put them to death; according to the commandment God had given him.

4 When Adam and Eve came to the eastern border of the garden--thinking in their hearts that the cherub was not watching--as they were standing by the gate as if wishing to go in, suddenly came the cherub with a flashing sword of fire in his hand; and when he saw them, he went forth to kill them. For he was afraid lest God should destroy him if they went into the garden without His order.

5 And the sword of the cherub seemed to flame afar off. But when he raised it over Adam and Eve, the flame thereof did not flash forth.

6 Therefore did the cherub think that God was favourable to them, and was bringing them back into the garden. And the cherub stood wondering.

7 He could not go up to Heaven to ascertain God's order regarding their getting into the garden; he therefore abode standing by them, unable as he was to part from them; for he was afraid lest they should enter the garden without leave from God, who then would destroy him.

8 When Adam and Eve saw the cherub coming towards them with a flaming sword of fire in his hand, they fell on their faces from fear, and were as dead.

9 At that time the heavens and the earth shook; and other cherubim came down from heaven to the cherub who guarded the garden, and saw him amazed and silent.

10 Then, again, other angels came down nigh unto the place where Adam and Eve were. They were divided between joy and sorrow.

11 They were glad, because they thought that God was favourable to Adam, and wished him to return to the garden; and wished to restore him to the gladness he once enjoyed.

12 But they sorrowed over Adam, because he was fallen like a dead man, he and Eve; and they said in their thoughts, "Adam has not died in this place; but God has put him to death, for his having come to this place, and wishing to get into the garden without His leave."

CHAP. LV.

The Conflict of Satan.

THEN came the Word of God to Adam and Eve, and raised them from their dead state, saying unto them, "Why came ye up hither? Dr, you intend to go into the garden, from which I brought you out? it can not be to-day; but only when the covenant I have made with you is fulfillled."

2 Then Adam, when he heard the Word of God, and the fluttering of the angels whom he did not see, but only heard the sound of them with his ears, he and Eve wept, and said to the angels:--

3 "O Spirits, who wait upon God, look upon me, and upon my being unable to see you! For when I was in my former bright nature) then I could see you. I sang praises as you do; and my heart was far above you.

4 "But now, that I have transgressed, that bright nature is gone from me, and I am come to this miserable state. And now am I come to this, that I cannot see you, and you do not serve me As you were wont. For I am become animal flesh.

5 "Yet now O angels of God, ask God with me, to restore me to that wherein I was formerly; to rescue me from this misery, and to remove from me the sentence of death He passed upon me, for having trespassed against Him."

6 Then, when the angels heard these words, they all grieved over him; and cursed Satan who had beguiled Adam, until he came from the garden to misery; from life to death; from peace to trouble; and from gladness to a strange land.

7 Then the angels said unto Adam, "Thou didst hearken to Satan, and didst forsake the Word of God who created thee; and thou didst believe that Satan would fulfill all he had promised thee.

8 "But now, O Adam, we will make known to thee, what came upon us through him, before his fall from heaven.

9 "He gathered together his hosts, and deceived them, promising them to give them a great kingdom, a divine nature; and other promises he made them.

10 "His hosts believed that. his word was true, so they yielded to him, and renounced the glory of God.

11 "He then sent for us according to the orders in which we were-to come under his command, and to hearken to his vain promise. But we would not, and we took not his advice.

12 "Then after he had fought with God, and had dealt forwardly with Him, he gathered together his hosts, and made war with us. And if it had not been for God's strength that was with us, we could not have prevailed against him to hurl him from heaven.

13 "But when he fell from among us, there was great joy in heaven, because of his going down from us. For had he continued in heaven, nothing, not even one angel would have remained in it.

14 "But God in His mercy, drove him from among us to this dark earth; for he had become darkness itself and a worker of unrighteousness.

15 "And he has continued, O Adam, to make war against thee, until he beguiled thee and made thee come out of the garden, to this strange land, where all these trials have come to thee. And death, which God brought upon him he has also brought to thee, O Adam, because thou didst obey him, and didst transgress against God."

16 Then a the angels rejoiced and praised God, and asked Him not to destroy Adam this time, for his having sought to enter the garden; but to bear with him until the fulfillment of the promise; and to help him in this world until he was free from Satan's hand.

CHAP. LVI.

A chapter of divine comfort.

THEN came the Word of God to Adam, and said unto him:--

2 "O Adam, look at that garden of joy and at this earth of toil, and behold the angels who are in the garden-that is full of them, and see thyself alone on this earth, with Satan whom thou didst obey.

3 "Yet, if thou hadst submitted, and been obedient to Me, and hadst kept My Word, thou wouldst be with My angels in My garden.

4 "But when thou didst transgress and hearken to Satan, thou didst become his guest among his angels, that are full of wickedness; and thou camest to this earth, that brings forth to thee thorns and thistles.

5 "O Adam, ask him who deceived thee, to give thee the divine nature he promised thee, or to make thee a garden as I had made for thee; or to fill thee with that same bright nature with which I had filled thee.

6 "Ask him to make thee a body like the one I made thee, or to give thee a day of rest as I gave thee; or to create within thee a reasonable soul, as I did create for thee; or to remove thee hence to some other earth than this one which I gave thee. But, O Adam, he will not fulfilll even one of the things he told thee.

7 "Acknowledge, then, My favour towards thee, and My mercy on thee, My creature; that I have not requited thee for thy transgression against Me, but in My pity for thee I have promised thee that at the end of the great five days and a half I will come and save thee."

8 Then God said again to Adam and Eve, "Arise, go down hence, lest the cherub with a sword of fire in his hand destroy you."

9 But Adam's heart was comforted by God's words to him, and he worshipped before Him.

10 And God commanded His angels to escort Adam and Eve to the cave with joy, instead of the fear that had come upon them.

11 Then the angels took up Adam and Eve, and brought them down from the mountain by the garden, with songs and psalms, until they brought them to the cave. There the angels began to comfort and to strengthen them, and then departed from them towards heaven, to their Creator, who had sent them.

12 But, after the angels were gone from Adam and Eve, came Satan, with shamefacedness, and stood at the entrance of the cave in which were Adam and Eve. He then called to Adam, and said, "O Adam, come, let me speak to thee."

13 Then Adam came out of the cave, thinking he was one of God's angels that was come to give him some good counsel.

CHAP. LVII.

"Therefore did I fall. . .

BUT when Adam came out and saw his hideous figure, he was afraid of him, and said unto him, "Who art thou?"

2 Then Satan answered and said unto him, "It is I, who hid myself within the serpent, and who talked to Eve, and beguiled her until she hearkened to my command. I am he who sent her, through the wiles of my speech, to deceive thee, until thou and she ate of the fruit of the tree, and ye came away from under the command of God."

3 But when Adam heard these words from him, he said unto him, "Canst thou make me a garden as God made for me? Or canst thou clothe me in the same bright nature in which God had clothed me?

4 "Where is the divine nature thou didst promise to give me? Where is that fair speech of thine, thou didst hold with us at first, when we were in the garden?"

5 Then Satan said unto Adam, "Thinkest thou, that when I have spoken to one about anything, I shall ever bring it to him or fulfill my word? Not so. For I myself have never even thought of obtaining what I asked.

6 "Therefore did I fall, and did I make you fall by that for which I myself fell; and with you also, whosoever accepts my counsel, falls thereby.

7 "But now, O Adam, by reason of thy fall thou art under my rule, and I am king over thee; because thou hast hearkened to me, and hast transgressed against thy God. Neither will there be any deliverance from my hands until the day promised thee by thy God."

8 Again he said, "Inasmuch as we do not know the day agreed upon with thee by thy God, nor the hour in which thou shalt be delivered, for that reason will we multiply war and murder upon thee and thy seed after thee.

9 "This is our will and our good pleasure, that we may not leave one of the sons of men to inherit our orders in heaven.

10 "For as to our abode, O Adam, it is in burning fire; and we will not cease our evil doing no, not one day nor one hour. And I, O Adam, shall sow fire upon thee when thou comest into the cave to dwell there."

11 When Adam heard these words he wept and mourned, and said unto Eve, "Hear what he said; that he will not fulfill aught of what he told thee in the garden. Did he really then become king over us?

12 "But we will ask God, who created us, to deliver us out of his hands."

CHAP. LVIII.

"About sunset on the 53rd day . . . ."

THEN Adam and Eve spread their hands unto God, praying and entreating Him to drive Satan away from them; that he do them no violence, and do not force them to deny God.

2 Then God sent to them at once His angel, who drove away Satan--from them. This happened about sunset, on the fifty-third day after they had come out of the garden.

3 Then Adam and Eve went into the cave, and stood up and turned their faces to the earth, to pray to God.

4 But ere they prayed Adam said unto Eve, "Lo, thou hast seen what temptations have befallen us in this land. Come, let us arise, and ask God to forgive us the sins we have committed; and we will not come out until the end of the day next to the fortieth. And if we die herein, He will save us."

5 Then Adam and Eve arose, and joined together in entreating God.

6 They abode thus praying in the cave; neither did they come out of it, by night or by day, until their prayers went up out of their mouths, like a flame of fire.

CHAP. LIX.

Eighth apparition of Satan to Adam and Eve.

BUT Satan, the hater of all good, did not allow them to end their prayers. For he called to his hosts, and they came, all of them. He then said to them, "Since Adam and Eve, whom we beguiled, have agreed together to pray to God night and day, and to entreat Him to deliver them, and since they will not come out of the cave until the end of the fortieth day.

2 "And since they will continue their prayers as they have both agreed to do, that He will deliver them out of our hands, and restore them to their former state, see what we shall do unto them." And his hosts said unto him, "Power is thine, O our Lord, to do what thou listest."

3 Then Satan, great in wickedness, took his hosts and came into the cave, in the thirtieth night of the forty days and one; and he smote Adam and Eve, until he left them dead.

4 Then came the Word of God unto Adam and Eve, who raised them from their suffering, and God said unto Adam, "Be strong, and be not afraid of him who has just come to thee."

5 But Adam wept and said, "Where wast Thou, O my God, that they should smite me with such blows, and that this suffering should come upon us; upon me and upon Eve, Thy handmaid?"

6 Then God said unto him, "O Adam, see, he is lord and master of all thou hast, he who said, he would give thee divinity. Where is this love for thee? And where is the gift he promised?

7 "For once has it pleased him, O Adam, to come to thee, to comfort thee, and to strengthen thee, and to rejoice with thee, and to send his hosts to guard thee; because thou hast hearkened to him, and hast yielded to his counsel; and hast transgressed My commandment but has followed his behest?"

8 Then Adam wept before the Lord, and said, "O Lord because I transgressed a little, Thou hast sorely plagued me in return for it, I ask Thee to deliver me out of his hands; or else have pity on me, and take my soul out of my body now in this strange land."

9 Then God said unto Adam, "If only there had been this sighing and praying before, ere thou didst transgress! Then wouldst thou have rest from the trouble in which thou art now."

10 But God had patience with Adam, and let him and Eve remain in the cave until they had fulfillled the forty days.

11 But as to Adam and Eve, their strength and flesh withered from fasting and praying, from hunger and thirst; for they had not tasted either food or drink since they left the garden; nor were the functions of their bodies yet settled; and they had no strength left to continue in prayer from hunger, until the end of the next day to the fortieth. They were fallen down in the cave; yet what speech escaped from their mouths, was only in praises.

CHAP. LX.

The Devil appears like an old man. He offers "a place of rest."

THEN on the eighty-ninth day, Satan came to the cave, clad in a garment of light, and girt about with a bright girdle.

2 In his hands was a staff of light, and he looked most awful: but his face was pleasant and his speech was sweet,

3 He thus transformed himself in order to deceive Adam and Eve, and to make them come out of the cave, ere they had fulfillled the forty days.

4 For he said within himself, "Now that when they had fulfillled the forty days' fasting and praying, God would restore them to their former estate; but if He did not do so, He would still be favourable to them; and even if He had not mercy on them, would He yet give them something from the garden to comfort them; as already twice before."

5 Then Satan drew near the cave in this fair appearance, and said:--

6 "O Adam, rise ye, stand up, thou and Eve, and come along with me, to a good land; and fear not. I am flesh and bones like you; and at first I was a creature that God created.

7 "And it was so, that when He had created me, He placed me in a garden in the north, on the border of the world.

8 "And He said to me, 'Abide here!' And I abode there according to His Word, neither did I transgress His commandment.

9 "Then He made a slumber to come over me, and He brought thee, O Adam, out of my side, but did not make thee abide by me.

10 "But God took thee in His divine hand, and placed thee in a garden to the eastward.

11 "Then I grieved because of thee, for that while God had taken thee out of my side, He had not let thee abide with me.

12 "But God said unto me: 'Grieve not because of Adam, whom I brought out of thy side; no harm will come to him.

13 "'For now I have brought out of his side a help-meet for him; and I have given him joy by so doing.'"

14 Then Satan said again, "I did not know how it is ye are in this cave, nor anything about this trial that has come upon you-until God said to me, 'Behold, Adam has transgressed, he whom I had taken out of thy side, and Eve also, whom I took out of his side; and I have driven them out of the garden; I have made them dwell in a land of sorrow and misery, because they transgressed against Me, and have hearkened to Satan. And lo, they are in suffering unto this day, the eightieth.'

15 "Then God said unto me, 'Arise, go to them, and make them come to thy place, and suffer not that Satan come near them, and afflict them. For they are now in great misery; and lie helpless from hunger.'

16 "He further said to me, 'When thou hast taken them to thyself, give them to eat of the fruit of the Tree of Life, and give them to drink of the water of peace; and clothe them in a garment of light, and restore them to their former state of grace, and leave them not in misery, for they came from thee. But grieve not over them, nor repent of that which has come upon them.'

17 "But when I heard this, I was sorry; and my heart could not patiently bear it for thy sake, O my child.

18 "But, O Adam, when I heard the name of Satan, I was afraid, and I said within myself, I will not come out, lest he ensnare me, as he did my children, Adam and Eve.

19 "And I said, 'O God, when I go to my children, Satan will meet me in the way, and war against me, as he did against them.'

20 "Then God said unto me, 'Fear not; when thou findest him, smite him with the staff that is in thine hand, and be not afraid of him for thou art of old standing, and he shall not prevail against thee.'

21 "Then I said, 'O my Lord, I am old, and cannot go. Send Thy angels to bring them.'

22 "But God said unto me, 'Angels, verily, are not like them; and they will not consent to come with them. But I have chosen thee, because they are thy offspring, and like thee, and will hearken to what thou sayest.'

23 "God said further to me, 'If thou hast not strength to walk, I will send a cloud to carry thee and alight thee at the entrance of their cave; then the cloud will return and leave thee there.

24 "'And if they will come with thee, I will send a cloud to carry thee and them.'

25 "Then He commanded a cloud, and it bare me up and brought me to you; and then went back.

26 "And now O my children, Adam and Eve, look at my hoar hairs and at my feeble estate, and at my coming from that distant place. Come, come with me, to a place of rest."

27 Then he began to weep and to sob before Adam and Eve, and his tears poured upon the earth like water.

28 And when Adam and Eve raised their eyes and saw his beard, and heard his sweet talk, their hearts softened towards him; they hearkened unto him, for they believed he was true.

29 And it seemed to them that they really were his offspring, when they saw that his face was like their own; and they trusted him.

CHAP. LXI.

They begin to follow Satan.

THEN he took Adam and Eve by the hand, and began to bring them out of the cave.

2 But when they were come a little way out of it, God knew that Satan had overcome them, and had brought them out ere the forty days were ended, to take them to some distant place, and to destroy them.

3 Then the Word of the Lord God again came and cursed Satan, and drove him away from them.

4 And God began to speak unto Adam and Eve, saying to them, "What made you come out of the cave, unto this place?"

5 Then Adam said unto God, "Didst thou create a man before us? For when we were in the cave there suddenly came unto us a good old man who said to us, 'I am a messenger from God unto you, to bring you back to some place of rest.'

6 "And we did believe, O God, that he was a messenger from Thee; and we came out with him; and knew not whither we should go with him."

7 Then God said unto Adam, "See, that is the father of evil arts, who brought thee and Eve out of the Garden of Delights. And now, indeed, when he saw that thou and Eve both joined together in fasting and praying, and that you came not out of the cave before the end of the forty days, he wished to make your purpose vain, to break your mutual bond; to cut off all hope from you, and to drive you to some place where he might destroy you.

8 "Because he was unable to do aught to you, unless he showed himself in the likeness of you.

9 "Therefore did he come to you with a face like your own, and began to give you tokens as if they were all true.

10 "But I in mercy and with the favour I had unto you, did not allow him to destroy you; but I drove him away from you.

11 "Now, therefore, O Adam, take Eve, and return to your cave, and remain in it until the morrow of the fortieth day. And when ye come out, go towards the eastern gate of the garden."

12 Then Adam and Eve worshipped God, and praised and blessed Him for the deliverance that had come to them from Him. And they returned towards the cave. This happened at eventide of the thirty-ninth day.

13 Then Adam and Eve stood up and with great zeal, prayed to God, to be brought out of their want for strength; for their strength had departed from them, through hunger and thirst and prayer. But they watched the whole of that night praying, until morning.

14 Then Adam said unto Eve, "Arise, let us go towards the eastern gate of the garden as God told us."

15 And they said their prayers as they were wont to do every day; and they went out of the cave, to go near to the eastern gate of the garden.

16 Then Adam and Eve stood up and prayed, and besought God to strengthen them, and to send them something to satisfy their hunger.

17 But when they had ended their prayers, they remained where they were by reason of their failing strength.

18. Then came the Word of God again, and said unto them, "O Adam, arise, go and bring hither two figs."

19 Then Adam and Eve arose, and went until they drew near to the cave.

CHAP. LXII.

Two fruit trees.

BUT Satan the wicked was envious, because of the consolation God had given them.

2 So he prevented them, and went into the cave and took the two figs, and buried them outside the cave, so that Adam and Eve should not find them. He also had in his thoughts to destroy them.

3 But by God's mercy, as soon as those two figs were in the earth, God defeated Satan's counsel regarding them; and made them into two fruit-trees, that overshadowed the cave. For Satan had buried them on the eastern side of it.

4 Then when the two trees were grown, and were covered with fruit, Satan grieved and mourned, and said, "Better were it to have left those figs as they were; for now, behold, they have become two fruit-trees, whereof Adam will eat all the days of his life. Whereas I had in mind, when I buried them, to destroy them entirely, and to hide them for aye.

5 "But God has overturned my counsel; and would not that this sacred fruit should perish; and He has made plain my intention, and has defeated the counsel I had formed against His servants."

6 Then Satan went away ashamed, of not having wrought out his design.

CHAP. LXIII

The first joy of trees.

BUT Adam and Eve, as they drew near to the cave, saw two fig-trees, covered with fruit, and overshadowing the cave.

2 Then Adam said to Eve, "It seems to me we have gone astray. When did these two trees grow here? It seems to me that the enemy wishes to lead us astray, Sayest thou that there is in the earth another cave than this?

3 "Yet, O Eve, let us go into the cave, and find in it the two figs; for this is our cave, in which we were. But if we should not find the two figs in it, then it cannot be our cave."

4 They went then into the cave, and looked into the four corners of it, but found not the two figs.

5 And Adam wept and said to Eve, "Are we come to a wrong cave, then, O Eve? It seems to me these two fig-trees are the two figs that were in the cave." And Eve said, "I, for my part, do not know."

6 Then Adam stood up and prayed and said, "O God, Thou didst command us to come back to the cave, to take the two figs, and then to return to Thee.

7 "But now, we have not found them. O God, hast Thou taken them, and sown these two trees, or have we gone astray in the earth; or has the enemy deceived us? If it be real, then, O God, reveal to us the secret of these two trees and of the two figs."

8 Then came the Word of God to Adam, and said unto him, "O Adam, when I sent thee to fetch the figs, Satan went before thee to the cave, took the figs, and buried them outside, eastward of the cave, thinking to destroy them; and not sowing them with good intent.

9 "Not for his mere sake, then, have these trees grown up at once; but I had mercy on thee and I commanded them to grow. And they grew to be two large trees, that you be overshadowed by their branches, and find rest; and that I make you see My power and My marvellous works.

10 "And, also, to show you Satan's meanness, and his evil works, for ever since ye came out of the garden, he has not ceased, no, not one day, from doing you some harm. But I have not given him power over you."

11 And God said, "Henceforth, O Adam, rejoice on account of the trees, thou and Eve; and rest under them when ye feel weary. But eat not of their fruit, nor come near them."

12 Then Adam wept, and said, "O God, wilt Thou again kill us, or wilt Thou drive us away from before Thy face, and cut our life from off the face of the earth?

13 "O God, I beseech Thee, if Thou knowest that there be in these trees either death or some other evil, as at the first time, root them up from near our cave, and wither them; and leave us to die of the heat, of hunger and of thirst.

14 "For we know Thy marvellous works, O God, that they are great, and that by Thy power Thou canst bring one thing out of another, without one's wish. For Thy power can make rocks to become trees, and trees to become rocks."

CHAP. LXIV.

Adam and Eve partake of the first earthly food.

THEN God looked upon Adam and upon his strength of mind, upon his
endurance of hunger and thirst, and of the heat. And he changed the two fig-trees
into two figs, as they were at first, and then said to Adam and to Eve, "Each of
you may take one fig." And they took them, as the Lord commanded them.

2 And he said to them, "Go ye into the cave, and eat the figs, and satisfy your hunger, lest ye die."

3 So, as God commanded them, they went into the cave, about the time when the sun was setting. And Adam and Eve stood up and prayed at the time of the setting sun.

4 Then they sat down to eat the figs; but they knew not how to eat them; for they were not accustomed to eat earthly food. They feared also lest, if they ate, their stomach should be burdened and their flesh thickened, and their hearts take to liking earthly food.

5 But while they were thus seated, God, out of pity for them, sent them His angel, lest they should perish of hunger and thirst.

6 And the angel said unto Adam and Eve, "God says to you that ye have not strength to fast until death; eat, therefore, and strengthen your bodies; for ye are now animal flesh, that cannot subsist without food and drink."

7 Then Adam and Eve took the figs and began to eat of them. But God had put into them a mixture as of savoury bread and blood.

8 Then the angel went from Adam and Eve, who ate of the figs until they had satisfied their hunger. Then they put by what remained; but by the power of God, the figs became full as before, because God blessed them.

9 After this Adam and Eve arose, and prayed with a joyful heart and renewed strength, and praised and rejoiced abundantly the whole of that night. And this was the end of the eighty-third day.

CHAP. LXV.

Adam and Eve acquire digestive organs. Final hope of returning to the Garden is quenched.

AND when it was day, they rose and prayed, after their custom, and then went out of the cave.

2 But as they felt great trouble from the food they had eaten, and to which they were not used, they went about in the cave saying to each other:--

3 "What has happened to us through eating, that this pain should have come upon us? Woe be to us, we shall die! Better for us to have died than to have eaten; and to have kept our bodies pure, than to have defiled them with food."

4 Then Adam said to Eve, "This pain did not come to us in the garden, neither did we eat such bad food there. Thinkest thou, O Eve, that God will plague us through the food that is in us, or that our inwards will come out; or that God means to kill us with this pain before He has fulfillled His promise to us?"

5 Then Adam besought the Lord and said, "O Lord, let us not perish through the food we have eaten. O Lord, smite us not; but deal with us according to Thy great mercy, and forsake us not until the day of the promise Thou hast made us."

6 Then God looked upon them, and at once fitted them for eating food; as unto this day; so that they should not perish.

7 Then Adam and Eve came back into the cave sorrowful and weeping because of the alteration in their nature. And they both knew from that hour that they were altered beings, that their hope of returning to the garden was now cut off; and that they could not enter it.

8 For that now their bodies had strange functions; and all flesh that requires food and drink for its existence, cannot be in the garden.

9 Then Adam said to Eve, "Behold, our hope is now cut off; and so is our trust to enter the garden. We no longer belong to the inhabitants of the garden; but henceforth we are earthy and of the dust, and of the inhabitants of the earth, We shall not return to the garden, until the day in which God has promised to save us, and to bring us again into the garden, as He promised us."

10 Then they prayed to God that He would have mercy on them; after which, their mind was quieted, their hearts were broken, and their longing was cooled down; and they were like strangers on earth. That night Adam and Eve spent in the cave, where they slept heavily by reason of the food they had eaten.

CHAP. LXVI.

Adam does his first day's work.

WHEN it was morning, the day after they had eaten food, Adam and Eve prayed in the cave, and Adam said unto Eve, "Lo, we asked for food of God, and He gave it. But now let us also ask Him to give us a drink of water."

2 Then they arose, and went to the bank of the stream of water, that was on the south border of the garden, in which they had before thrown themselves. And they stood on the bank, and prayed to God that He would command them to drink of the water.

3 Then the Word of God came to Adam, and said unto him, "O Adam, thy body is become brutish, and requires water to drink. Take ye, and drink, thou and Eve; give thanks and praise."

4 Adam and Eve then drew near, and drank of it, until their bodies felt refreshed. After having drunk, they praised God, and then returned to their cave, after their former custom. This happened at the end of eighty-three days.

5 Then on the eighty-fourth day, they took two figs and hung them in the cave, together with the leaves thereof, to be to them a sign and a blessing from God. And they placed them there until there should arise a posterity to them, who should see the wonderful things God had done to them.

6 Then Adam and Eve again stood outside the cave, and besought God to show them some food wherewith to nourish their bodies.

7 Then the Word of God came and said unto him, "O Adam, go down to the westward of the cave, as far as a land of dark soil, and there thou shalt find food."

8 And Adam hearkened unto the Word of God, took Eve, and went down to a land of dark soil, and found there wheat growing, in the ear and ripe, and figs to eat; and Adam rejoiced over it.

9 Then the Word of God came again to Adam, and said unto him, "Take of this wheat and make thee bread of it, to nourish thy body withal." And God gave Adam's heart wisdom, to work out the corn until it became bread.

10 Adam accomplished all that, until he grew very faint and weary. He then returned to the cave; rejoicing at what he had learned of what is done with wheat, until it is made into bread for one's use.

CHAP. LXVII.

"Then Satan began to lead astray Adam and Eve. . . ."

BUT when Adam and Eve went down to the land of black mud, and came near to the wheat God had showed them, and saw it ripe and ready for reaping, as they had no sickle to reap it withal--they girt themselves, and began to pull up the wheat, until it was all done.

2 Then they made it into a heap; and, faint from heat and from thirst, they went under a shady tree, where the breeze fanned them to sleep.

3 But Satan saw what Adam and Eve had done. And he called his hosts, and said to them, "Since God has shown to Adam and Eve all about this wheat, wherewith to strengthen their bodies--and, lo, they are come and have made a heap of it, and faint from the toil are now asleep--come, let us set fire to this heap of corn, and burn it, and let us take that bottle of water that is by them, and empty it out, so that they may find nothing to drink, and we kill them with hunger and thirst.

4 "Then, when they wake up from their sleep, and seek to return to the cave, we will come to them in the way, and will lead them astray; so that they die of hunger and thirst; when they may, perhaps, deny God, and He destroy them. So shall we be rid of them."

5 Then Satan and his hosts threw fire upon the wheat and consumed it.

6 But from the heat of the flame Adam and Eve awoke from their sleep, and saw the wheat burning, and the bucket of water by them, poured out.

7 Then they wept and went back to the cave.

8 But as they were going up from below the mountain where they were, Satan and his hosts met them in the form of angels, praising God.

9 Then Satan said to Adam, "O Adam, why art thou so pained with hunger and thirst? It seems to me that Satan has burnt up the wheat." And Adam said to him, "Ay."

10 Again Satan said to Adam, "Come back with us; we are angels of God. God sent us to thee, to show thee another field of corn, better than that; and beyond it

is a fountain of good water, and many trees, where thou shalt dwell near it, and work the corn-field to better purpose than that which Satan has consumed."

11 Adam thought that he was true, and that they were angels who talked with him; and he went back with them.

12. Then Satan began to lead astray Adam and Eve eight days, until they both fell down as if dead, from hunger, thirst, and faintness. Then he fled with his hosts, and left them.

CHAP. LXVIII.

How destruction and trouble is of Satan when he is the master. Adam and Eve establish the custom of worship.

THEN God looked upon Adam and Eve, and upon what had come upon them from Satan, and how he had made them perish.

2 God, therefore, sent His Word, and raised up Adam and Eve from their state of death.

3 Then, Adam, when he was raised, said, "O God, Thou hast burnt and taken from us the corn Thou hadst given us, and Thou hast emptied out the bucket of water. And Thou hast sent Thy angels, who have waylaid us from the corn-field. Wilt Thou make us perish? If this be from Thee, O God, then take away our souls; but punish us not."

4 Then God said to Adam, "I did not burn down the wheat, and I did not pour the water out of the bucket, and I did not send My angels to lead thee astray.

5 "But it is Satan, thy master who did it; he to whom thou hast subjected thyself; My commandment being meanwhile set aside. He it is, who burnt down the corn, and poured out the water, and who has led thee astray; and all the promises he has made you, verily are but feint, and deceit, and a lie.

6 "But now, O Adam, thou shalt acknowledge My good deeds done to thee."

7 And God told His angels to take Adam and Eve, and to bear them up to the field of wheat, which they found as before, with the bucket full of water.

8 There they saw a tree, and found on it solid manna; and wondered at God's power. And the angels commanded them to eat of the manna when they were hungry.

9 And God adjured Satan with a curse, not to come again, and destroy the field of corn.

10 Then Adam and Eve took of the corn, and made of it an offering, and took it and offered it up on the mountain, the place where they had offered up their first offering of blood.

11 And they offered this oblation again on the altar they had built at first. And they stood up and prayed, and besought the Lord saying, "Thus, O God, when we were in the garden, did our praises go up to Thee, like this offering; and our innocence went up to thee like incense. But now, O God, accept this offering from us, and turn us not back, reft of Thy mercy."

12 Then God said to Adam and Eve, "Since ye have made this oblation and have offered it to Me, I shall make it My flesh, when I come down upon earth to save you; and I shall cause it to be offered continually upon an altar, for forgiveness and for mercy, unto those who partake of it duly."

13 And God sent a bright fire upon the offering of Adam and Eve, and filled it with brightness, grace, and light; and the Holy Ghost came down upon that oblation.

14 Then God commanded an angel to take fire-tongs, like a spoon, and with it to take an offering and bring it to Adam and Eve. And the angel did so, as God had commanded him, and offered it to them.

15 And the souls of Adam and Eve were brightened, and their hearts were filled with joy and gladness and with the praises of God.

16 And God said to Adam, "This shall be unto you a custom, to do so, when affliction and sorrow come upon you. But your deliverance and your entrance into the garden, shall not be until the days are fulfillled, as agreed between you and Me; were it not so, I would, of My mercy and pity for you, bring you back to My garden and to My favour for the sake of the offering you have just made to My name."

17 Adam rejoiced at these words which he heard from God; and he and Eve worshipped before the altar, to which they bowed, and then went back to the Cave of Treasures.

18 And this took place at the end of the twelfth day after the eightieth day, from the time Adam and Eve came out of the garden.

19 And they stood up the whole night praying until morning; and then went out of the cave.

20 Then Adam said to Eve, with joy of heart, because of the offering they had made to God, and that had been accepted of Him, "Let us do this three times every week, on the fourth day Wednesday, on the preparation day Friday, and on the Sabbath Sunday, all the days of our life."

21 And as they agreed to these words between themselves, God was pleased with their thoughts, and with the resolution they had each taken with the other.

22 After this, came the Word of God to Adam, and said, "O Adam, thou hast determined beforehand the days in which sufferings shall come upon Me, when I am made flesh; for they are the fourth Wednesday, and the preparation day Friday.

23 "But as to the first day, I created in it all things, and I raised the heavens. And, again, through My rising again on this day, will I create joy, and raise them on high, who believe in Me; O Adam, offer this oblation, all the days of thy life."

24 Then God withdrew His Word from Adam.

25 But Adam continued to offer this oblation thus, every week three times, until, the end of seven weeks. And on the first day, which is the fiftieth, Adam made an offering as he was wont, and he and Eve took it and came to the altar before God, as He had taught them.

CHAP. LXIX.

 Twelfth apparition of Satan to Adam and Eve, while Adam was praying over the offering upon the altar; when Satan smote him.

[91]

THEN Satan, the hater of all good, envious of Adam and of his offering through which he found favour with God, hastened and took a sharp stone from among sharp iron-stones; appeared in the form of a man, and went and stood by Adam and Eve.

2 Adam was then offering on the altar, and had begun to pray, with his hands spread unto God.

3 Then Satan hastened with the sharp iron-stone he had with him, and with it pierced Adam on the right side, when flowed blood and water, then Adam fell upon the altar like a corpse. And Satan fled.

4 Then Eve came, and took Adam and placed him below the altar. And there she stayed, weeping over him; while a stream of blood flowed from Adam's side upon his offering.

5 But God looked upon the death of Adam. He then sent His Word, and raised him up and said unto him, "Fulfill thy offering, for indeed, Adam, it is worth much, and there is no shortcoming in it."

6 God said further unto Adam, "Thus will it also happen to Me, on the earth, when I shall be pierced and blood shall flow blood and water from My side and run over My body, which is the true offering; and which shall be offered on the altar as a perfect offering."

7 Then God commanded Adam to finish his offering, and when he had ended it he worshipped before God, and praised Him for the signs He had showed him.

8 And God healed Adam in one day, which is the end of the seven weeks; and that is the fiftieth day.

9 Then Adam and Eve returned from the mountain, and went into the Cave of Treasures, as they were used to do. This completed for Adam and Eve, one hundred and forty days since their coming out of the garden.

10 Then they both stood up that night and prayed to God. And when it was morning, they went out, and went down westward of the cave, to the place where their corn was, and there rested under the shadow of a tree, as they were wont.

11 But when there a multitude of beasts came all round them. It was Satan's doing, in his wickedness; in order to wage war against Adam through marriage.

[93]

CHAP. LXX.

Thirteenth apparition of Satan to Adam and Eve, to make war against him, through his marriage with Eve.

AFTER this Satan, the hater of all good, took the form n angel, and with him two others, so that they looked like the three angels who had brought to Adam gold, incense, and myrrh.

2 They passed before Adam and Eve while they were under the tree, and greeted Adam and Eve with fair words that were full of guile.

3 But when Adam and Eve saw their comely mien, and heard their sweet speech, Adam rose, welcomed them, and brought them to Eve, and they remained all together; Adam's heart the while, being glad because he thought concerning them, that they were the same angels, who had brought him gold, incense, and myrrh.

4 Because, when they came to Adam the first time, there came upon him from them, peace and joy, through their bringing him good tokens; so Adam thought that they were come a second time to give him other tokens for him to rejoice withal. For he did not know it was Satan; therefore did he receive them with joy and companied with them.

5 Then Satan, the tallest of them, said, "Rejoice, O Adam, and be glad. Lo, God has sent us to thee to tell thee something."

6 And Adam said, "What is it?" Then Satan answered, "It is a light thing, yet it is a word of God, wilt thou hear it from us and do it? But if thou hearest not, we will return to God, and tell Him that thou wouldest not receive His word."

And Satan said again to Adam, "Fear not, neither let a trembling come upon thee; dost not thou know us?"

8 But Adam said, "I know you not."

9 Then Satan said to him, "I am the angel who brought thee gold, and took it to the cave; this other one is he who brought thee incense; and that third one, is he who brought thee myrrh when thou wast on the top of the mountain, and who carried thee to the cave.

10 "But as to the other angels our fellows, who bare you to the cave, God has not sent them with us this time; for He said to us, 'You suffice.'"

11 So when Adam heard these words he believed them, and said to these angels, "Speak the word of God, that I may receive it."

12 And Satan said unto him "Swear, and promise me that thou wilt receive it."

13 Then Adam said, "I know not how to swear and promise."

14 And Satan said to him, "Hold out thy hand, and put it inside my hand."

15 Then Adam held out his hand, and put it into Satan's hand; when Satan said unto him, "Say, now--so true as God is living, rational, and speaking, who raised the heavens in the space, and established the earth upon the waters, and has created me out of the four elements, and out of the dust of the earth--I will not break my promise, nor renounce my word."

16 And Adam swore thus.

17 Then Satan said to him, "Lo, it is now some time since thou camest out of the garden, and thou knowest neither wickedness nor evil. But now God s says to thee, to take Eve who came out of thy side, and to wed her, that she bear thee children, to comfort thee, and to drive from thee trouble and sorrow; now this thing is not difficult, neither is there any scandal in it to thee."

CHAP. LXXI.

Adam is troubled by his wedding with Eve.

BUT when Adam heard these words from Satan, he sorrowed much, because of his oath and of his promise, and said, "Shall I commit adultery with my flesh and my bones, and shall I sin against myself, for God to destroy me, and to blot me out from off the face of the earth?

2 "Since, when at first, I ate of the tree, He drove me out of the garden into this strange land, and deprived me of my bright nature, and brought death upon me. If, then, I should do this, He will cut off my life from the earth, and He will cast me into hell, and will plague me there a long time.

3 "But God never spoke the words thou hast told me; and ye are not God's angels, nor yet sent from Him. But ye are devils, come to me under the false appearance of angels . Away from me; ye cursed of God!"

4 Then those devils fled from before Adam. And he and Eve arose, and returned to the Cave of Treasures, and went into it.

5 Then Adam said to Eve, "If thou sawest what I did, tell it not; for I sinned against God n swearing by His great name, and I have placed my hand another time into that of Satan." Eve, then, held her peace, as Adam told her.

6 Then Adam arose, and spread his hands unto God, beseeching and entreating Him with tears, to forgive him what he had done. And Adam remained thus standing and praying forty days and forty nights. He neither ate nor drank until he dropped down upon the earth from hunger and thirst.

7 Then God sent His Word unto Adam, who raised him up from where he lay, and said unto him, "O Adam, why hast thou sworn by My name, and why hast thou made agreement with Satan another time?"

8 But Adam wept, and said, "O God, forgive me, for I did this unwittingly; believing they were God's angels."

9 And God forgave Adam, saying, to him, "Beware of Satan."

10 And He withdrew His Word from Adam.

11 Then Adam's heart was comforted; and he took Eve, and they went out of the cave, to make some food for their bodies.

12 But from that day Adam struggled in his mind about his wedding Eve; afraid as he was to do it, lest God should be wroth with him.

13 Then Adam and Eve went to the river of water, and sat on the bank, as people do when they enjoy themselves.

14 But Satan was jealous of them; and would destroy them.

CHAP. LXXII.

Adam's heart is set on fire.

THEN Satan, and ten from his hosts, transformed themselves into maidens, unlike any others in the whole world for grace.

2 They came up out of the river in presence of Adam and Eve, and they said among themselves, "Come, we will look at the faces of Adam and of Eve, who are of the men upon earth. How beautiful they are, and how different is their look from our own faces." Then they came to Adam and Eve, and greeted them; and stood wondering at them.

3 Adam and Eve looked at them also, and wondered at their beauty, and said, "Is there, then, under us, another world, with such beautiful creatures as these in it'"

4 And those maidens said to Adam and Eve, "Yes, indeed, we are an abundant creation."

5 Then Adam said to them, "But how do you multiply?"

6 And they answered him, "We have husbands who wedded us, and we bear them children, who grow up, and who in their turn wed and are wedded, and also bear children; and thus we increase. And if so be, O Adam, thou wilt not believe us, we will show thee our husbands and our children."

7 Then they shouted over the river as if to call their husbands and their children, who came up from the river, men and children; and every one came to his wife, his children being with him.

8 But when Adam and Eve saw them, they stood dumb, and wondered at them.

9 Then they said to Adam and Eve, "You see our husbands and our children, wed Eve as we wed our wives, and you shall have children the same as we." This was a device of Satan to deceive Adam.

10 Satan also thought within himself, "God at first commanded Adam concerning the fruit of the tree, saying to him, 'Eat not of it; else of death thou shalt die.' But Adam ate of it, and yet God did not kill him; He only decreed upon him death, and plagues and trials, until the day he shall come out of his body.

11 "Now, then, if I deceive him to do this thing, and to wed Eve without God's commandment, God will kill him then."

12 Therefore did Satan work this apparition before Adam and Eve; because he sought to kill him, and to make him disappear from off the face of the earth.

13 Meanwhile the fire of sin came upon Adam, and he thought of committing sin. But he restrained himself, fearing lest if he followed this advice of Satan God would put him to death.

14 Then Adam and Eve arose, and prayed to God, while Satan and his hosts went down into the river, in presence of Adam and Eve; to let them see that they were going back to their own regions.

15 Then Adam and Eve went back to the Cave of Treasures, as they were wont; about evening time.

16 And they both arose and prayed to God that night. Adam remained standing in prayer, yet not knowing how to pray, by reason of the thoughts of his heart regarding his wedding Eve; and he continued so until morning.

17 And when light arose, Adam said unto Eve, "Arise, let us go below the mountain, where they brought us gold, and let us ask the Lord concerning this matter."

18 Then Eve said, "What is that matter, O Adam?"

19 And he answered her, "That I may request the Lord to inform me about wedding thee; for I will not do it without His order, lest He make us perish, thee and me. For those devils have set my heart on fire, with thoughts of what they showed us, in their sinful apparitions."

20 Then Eve said to Adam, "Why need we go below the mountain? Let us rather stand up and pray in our cave to God, to let us know whether this counsel is good or not."

21 Then Adam rose up in prayer and said, "O God, thou knowest that we transgressed against Thee, and from the moment we transgressed, we were bereft of our bright nature; and our body became brutish, requiring food and drink; and with animal desires.

22 "Command us, O God, not to give way to them without Thy order, lest Thou bring us to nothing. For if Thou give us not the order, we shall be overpowered, and follow that advice of Satan; and Thou wilt again make us perish.

23 "If not, then take our souls from us; let us be rid of this animal lust. And if Thou give us no order respecting this thing, then sever Eve from me, and me from her; and place us each far away from the other.

24 "Yet again, O God, when Thou hast put us asunder from each other, the devils will deceive us with their apparitions, and destroy our hearts, and defile our thoughts towards each other. Yet if it is not each of us towards the other, it will, at all events, be through their appearance when they show themselves to us." Here Adam ended his prayer.

CHAP. LXXIII.

 The betrothal of Adam and Eve.

THEN God looked upon the words of Adam that they were true, and that he could long await His order, respecting the counsel of Satan.

2 And God approved Adam in what he had thought concerning this, and in the prayer he had offered in His presence; and the Word of God came unto Adam and said to him, "O Adam, if only thou hadst had this caution at first, ere thou earnest out of the garden into this land!"

3 After that, God sent His angel who had brought gold, and the angel who had brought incense, and the angel who had brought myrrh to Adam, that they should inform him respecting his wedding Eve.

4 Then those angels said to Adam, "Take the gold and give it to Eve as a wedding gift, and betroth her; then give her some incense and myrrh as a present; and be ye, thou and she, one flesh."

5 Adam hearkened to the angels, and took the gold and put it into Eve's bosom in her garment; and bethrothed her with his hand.

6 Then the angels commanded Adam and Eve, to arise and pray forty days and forty nights; and after that, that Adam should come in to his wife; for then this

would be an act pure and undefiled; and he should have children who would multiply, and replenish the face of the earth.

7 Then both Adam and Eve received the words of the angels; and the angels departed from them.

8 Then Adam and Eve began to fast and to pray, until the end of the forty days; and then they came together, as the angels had told them. And from the time Adam left the garden until he wedded Eve, were two hundred and twenty-three days, that is seven months and thirteen days.

9 Thus was Satan's war with Adam defeated.

CHAP. LXXIV.

The birth of Cain and Luluwa. Why they received those names.

AND they dwelt on the earth working, in order to continue in the well-being of their bodies; and were so until the nine months of Eve's childbearing were ended, and the time drew near when she must be delivered.

2 Then she said unto Adam, "This cave is a pure spot by reason of the signs wrought in it since we left the garden; and we shall again pray in it. It is not meet, then, that I should bring forth in it; let us rather repair to that of the sheltering rock, which Satan hurled at us, when he wished to kill us with it; but that was held up and spread as an awning over us by the command of God; and formed a cave."

3 Then Adam removed Eve to that cave; and when the time came that she should bring forth, she travailed much. So was Adam sorry, and his heart suffered for her sake; for she was nigh unto death; that the word of God to her should be fulfillled: "In suffering shalt thou bear a child, and in sorrow shalt thou bring forth thy child."

4 But when Adam saw the strait in which Eve was, he arose and prayed to God, and said, "O Lord, look upon me with the eye of Thy mercy, and bring her out of her distress."

5 And God looked at His maid-servant Eve, and delivered her, and she brought forth her first-born son, and with him a daughter.

6 Then Adam rejoiced at Eve's deliverance, and also over the children she had borne him. And Adam ministered unto Eve in the cave, until the end of eight days; when they named the son Cain, and the daughter Luluwa.

7 The meaning of Cain is "hater," because he hated his sister in their mother's womb; ere they came out of it. Therefore did Adam name him Cain.

8 But Luluwa means "beautiful," because she was more beautiful than her mother.

9 Then Adam and Eve waited until Cain and his sister were forty days old, when Adam said unto Eve, "We will make an offering and offer it up in behalf of the children."

10 And Eve said, "We will make one offering for the firstborn son; and afterwards we shall make one for the daughter."

CHAP. LXXV.

The family revisits the Cave of Treasures. Birth of Abel and Aklemia.

THEN Adam prepared an offering, and he and Eve offered it up for their children, and brought it to the altar they had built at first.

2 And Adam offered up the offering, and besought God to accept his offering.

3 Then God accepted Adam's offering, and sent a light from heaven that shone upon the offering. And Adam and the son drew near to the offering, but Eve and the daughter did not approach unto it.

4 Then Adam came down from upon the altar, and they were joyful; and Adam and Eve waited until the daughter was eighty days old; then Adam prepared an offering and took it to Eve and to the children; and they went to the altar, where Adam offered it up, as he was wont, asking the Lord to accept his offering.

5 And the Lord accepted the offering of Adam and Eve. Then Adam, Eve, and the children, drew near together, and came down from the mountain, rejoicing.

6 But they returned not to the cave in which they were born; but came to the Cave of Treasures, in order that the children should go round it, and be blessed with the tokens brought from the garden.

7 But after they had been blessed with these tokens, they went back to the cave in which they were born.

8 However, before Eve had offered up the offering, Adam had taken her, and had gone with her to the river of water, in which they threw themselves at first; and there they washed themselves. Adam washed his body and Eve hers also clean, after the suffering and distress that had come upon them.

9 But Adam and Eve, after washing themselves in the river of water, returned every night to the Cave of Treasures, where they prayed and were blessed; and then went back to their cave where the children were born

10 So did Adam and Eve until the children had done sucking. Then, when they were weaned, Adam made an offering for the souls of his children; other than the three times he made an offering for them, every week.

11 When the days of nursing the children were ended, Eve again conceived, and when her days were accomplished she brought forth another son and daughter; and they named the son Abel, and the daughter Aklia.

12 Then at the end of forty days, Adam made an offering for the son, and at the end of eighty days he made another offering for the daughter, and did by them, as he had done before by Cain and his sister Luluwa.

13 He brought them to the Cave of Treasures, where they received a blessing, and then returned to the cave where they were born. After the birth of these, Eve ceased from childbearing.

CHAP. LXXVI.

Cain becomes jealous because of his sisters.

A ND the children began to wax stronger, and to grow in stature; but Cain was hardhearted, and ruled over his younger brother.

2 And oftentimes when his father made an offering, he would remain behind and not go with them, to offer up.

3 But, as to Abel, he had a meek heart, and was obedient to his father and mother, whom he often moved to make an offering, because he loved it; and prayed and fasted much.

4 Then came this sign to Abel. As he was coming into the Cave of Treasures, and saw the golden rods, the incense and the myrrh, he inquired of his parents Adam and Eve concerning them, and said unto them, "How did you come by these?"

5 Then Adam told him all that had befallen them. And Abel felt deeply about what his father told him.

6 Furthermore his father Adam, told him of the works of God, and of the garden; and after that, he remained behind his father the whole of that night in the Cave of Treasures.

7 And that night, while he was praying, Satan appeared unto him under the figure of a man, who said to him, "Thou hast oftentimes moved thy father to make an offering, to fast and to pray, therefore I will kill thee, and make thee perish from this world."

8 But as for Abel, he prayed to God, and drove away Satan from him; and believed not the words of the devil. Then when it was day, an angel of God appeared unto him, who said to him, "Shorten neither fasting, prayer, nor offering up an oblation unto thy God. For, lo, the Lord has accepted thy prayer. Be not afraid of the figure which appeared unto thee in the night, and who cursed thee unto death." And the angel departed from him.

9 Then when it was day, Abel came to Adam and Eve, and told them of the vision he had seen. But when they heard it, they grieved much over it, yet said nothing to him about it; they only comforted him.

10 But as to hard-hearted Cain, Satan came to him by night, showed himself and said unto him, "Since Adam and Eve love thy brother Abel much more than they love thee, and wish to join him in marriage to thy beautiful sister, because they love him; but wish to join thee in marriage to his ill-favoured sister, because they hate thee;

11 "Now, therefore, I counsel thee, when they do that, to kill thy brother; then thy sister will be left for thee; and his sister will be cast, away."

12 And Satan departed from him. But the wicked One remained behind in the heart of Cain, who sought many a time, to kill his brother.

CHAP. LXXVII.

Cain, 15 years old, and Abel 12 years old, grow apart.

BUT when Adam saw that the elder brother hated the younger, he endeavoured to soften their hearts, and said unto Cain, "Take, O my son, of the fruits of thy sowing, and make an offering unto God, that He may forgive thee thy wickedness and thy sin."

2 He said also to Abel, "Take thou of thy sowing and make an offering and bring it to God, that He may forgive thy wickedness and thy sin."

3 Then Abel hearkened unto his father's voice, and took of his sowing, and made a good offering, and said to his father, Adam, "Come with me, to show me how to offer it up."

4 And they went, Adam and Eve with him, and showed him how to offer up his gift upon the altar. Then after that, they stood up and prayed that God would accept Abel's offering.

5 Then God looked upon Abel and accepted his offering. And God was more pleased with Abel than with his offering, because of his good heart and pure body. There was no trace of guile in him.

6 Then they came down from the altar, and went to the cave in which they dwelt. But Abel, by reason of his joy at having made his offering, repeated it three times a week, after the example of his father Adam.

7 But as to Cain, he took no pleasure in offering; but after much anger on his father's part, he offered up his gift once; and when he did offer up, his eye was on the offering he made, and he took the smallest of his sheep for an offering, and his eye was again on it. '

8 Therefore God did not accept his offering, because his heart was full of murderous thoughts.

9 And they all thus lived together in the cave in which Eve had brought forth, until Cain was fifteen years old, and Abel twelve years old.

CHAP. LXXVIII.

Jealousy overcomes Cain. He makes trouble in the family. How the first murder was planned.

THEN Adam said to Eve, "Behold the children are grown up; we must think of finding wives for them."

2 Then Eve answered, "How can we do it?"

3 Then Adam said to her, "We will join Abel's sister in marriage to Cain, and Cain's sister to Abel."

4 Then said Eve to Adam, "I do not like Cain because he is hard-hearted; but let them bide until we offer up unto the Lord in their behalf."

5 And Adam said no more.

6 Meanwhile Satan came to Cain in the figure of a man of the field, and said to him, "Behold Adam and Eve have taken counsel together about the marriage of you two; and they have agreed to marry Abel's sister to thee, and thy sister to him.

7 "But if it was not that I love thee, I would not have told thee this thing. Yet if thou wilt take my advice, and hearken to me, I will bring: thee on thy wedding day beautiful robes, gold and silver in plenty, and my relations will attend thee."

8 Then Cain said with joy, "Where are thy relations?"

9 And Satan answered, "My relations are in a garden in the north, whither I once meant to bring thy father Adam; but he would not accept my offer.

10 "But thou, if thou wilt receive my words and if thou wilt come unto me after thy wedding, thou shalt rest from the misery in which thou art; and thou shalt rest and be better off than thy father Adam."

11 At these words of Satan Cain opened his ears, and leant towards his speech.

12 And he did not remain in the field, but he went to Eve, his mother, and beat her, and cursed her, and said to her, "Why are ye about taking my sister to wed her to my brother? Am I dead""

13 His mother, however, quieted him, and sent him to the field where be had been.

14 Then when Adam came, she told him of what Cain had done.

15 But Adam grieved and held his peace, and said not a word.

16 Then on the morrow Adam said unto Cain his son, "Take of thy sheep, young and good, and offer them up unto thy God; and I will speak to thy brother, to make unto his God an offering of corn."

17 They both hearkened to their father Adam, and they took their offerings, and offered them up on the mountain by the altar.

18 But Cain behaved haughtily towards his brother, and thrust him from the altar, and would not let him offer up his gift upon the altar; but he offered his own upon it, with a proud heart, full of guile, and fraud.

19 But as for Abel, he set up stones that were near at hand, and upon that, he offered up his gift with a heart humble and free from guile.

20 Cain was then standing by the altar on which he had offered up his gift; and he cried unto God to accept his offering; but God did not accept it from him; neither did a divine fire come down to consume his offering.

21 But he remained standing over against the altar, out of humour and wroth, looking towards his brother Abel, to see if God would accept his offering or not.

22 And Abel prayed unto God to accept his offering. Then a divine fire came down and consumed his offering. And God smelled the sweet savour of his offering; because Abel loved Him and rejoiced in Him.

23 And because God was well pleased with him He sent him an angel of light in the figure of man who had partaken of his offering, because He had smelled the sweet savour of his offering, and they comforted Abel and strengthened his heart.

24 But Cain was looking on all that took place at his brother's offering, and was wroth on account of it.

25 Then he opened his mouth and blasphemed God, because He had not accepted his offering.

26 But God said unto Cain, "Wherefore is thy countenance sad? Be righteous, that I may accept thy offering. Not against

Me hast thou murmured, but against thyself."

27 And God said this to Cain in rebuke, and because He abhorred him and his offering.

28 And Cain came down from the altar, his colour changed and of a woeful countenance, and came to his father and mother and told them all that had befallen him. And Adam grieved much because God had not accepted Cain's offering.

29 But Abel came down rejoicing, and with a gladsome heart, and told his father and mother how God had accepted his offering. And they rejoiced at it and kissed his face.

30 And Abel said to his father, "Because Cain thrust me from the altar, and would not allow me to offer my gift upon it, I made an altar for myself and offered my gift upon it."

31 But when Adam heard this he was very sorry, because it was the altar he had built at first, and upon which he had offered his own gifts.

32 As to Cain, he was so sullen and so angry that he went into the field, where Satan came to him and said to him, "Since thy brother Abel has taken refuge with thy father Adam, because thou didst thrust him from the altar, they have kissed his face, and they rejoice over him, far more than over thee."

33 When Cain heard these words of Satan, he was filled with rage; and he let no one know. But he was laying wait to kill his brother, until he brought him into the cave, and then said to him:--

34 "O brother, the country is so beautiful, and there are such beautiful and pleasurable trees in it, and charming to look at! But brother, thou hast never been one day in the field to take thy pleasure therein.

35 "To-day, O, my brother, I very much wish thou wouldest come with me into the field, to enjoy thyself and to bless our fields and our flocks, for thou art righteous, and I love thee much, O my brother! but thou hast estranged thyself from me."

36 Then Abel consented to go with his brother Cain into the field.

37 But before going out, Cain said to Abel, "Wait for me, until I fetch a staff, because of wild beasts."

38 Then Abel stood waiting in his innocence. But Cain, the forward, fetched a staff and went out.

39 And they began, Cain and his brother Abel, to walk in the way; Cain talking to him, and comforting him, to make him forget everything.

CHAP. LXXIX.

A wicked plan is carried to a tragic conclusion. Cain is frightened. "Am I my brother's keeper?" The seven punishments. Peace is shattered.

AND so they went on, until they came to a lonely place, where there were no sheep; then Abel said to Cain, "Behold, my brother, we are weary of walking; for we see none of the trees, nor of the fruits, nor of the verdure, nor of the sheep, nor any one of the things of which thou didst tell me. Where are those sheep of thine thou didst tell me to bless?"

2 Then Cain said to him, "Come on, and presently thou shalt see many beautiful things. but go before me, until I come up to thee."

3 Then went Abel forward, but Cain remained behind him.

4 And Abel was walking in his innocence, without guile; not believing his brother would kill him.

5 Then Cain, when he came up to him, comforted him with his talk, walking a little behind him; then he hastened, and smote him with the staff, blow upon blow, until he was stunned,

6 But when Abel fell down upon the ground, seeing that his brother meant to kill him, he said to Cain, "O, my brother, have pity on me. By the breasts we have sucked, smite me not! By the womb that bare us and that brought us into the world, smite me not unto death with that staff! If thou wilt kill me, take one of these large stones, and kill me outright."

7 Then Cain, the hard-hearted, and cruel murderer, took a large stone, and smote his brother with it upon the head, until his brains oozed out, and he weltered in his blood, before him.

8 And Cain repented not of what he had done.

9 But the earth, when the blood of righteous Abel fell upon it, trembled, as it drank his blood, and would have brought Cain to naught for it.

10 And the blood of Abel cried mysteriously to God, to avenge him of his murderer.

11 Then Cain began at once to dig the earth wherein to lay his brother; for he was trembling from the fear that came upon him, when he saw the earth tremble on his account.

12 He then cast his brother into the pit he made, and covered him with dust. But the earth would not receive him; but it threw him up at once.

13 Again did Cain dig the earth and hid his brother in it; but again did the earth throw him up on itself; until three times did the earth thus throw up on itself the body of Abel.

14 The muddy earth threw him up the first time, because he was not the first creation; and it threw him up the second time and would not receive him, because he was righteous and good, and was killed without a cause; and the earth threw him up the third time and would not receive him, that there might remain before his brother a witness against him.

15 And so did the earth mock Cain, until the Word of God, came to him concerning his brother.

16 Then was God angry, and much displeased at Abel's death; and He thundered from heaven, and lightnings went before Him, and the Word of the Lord God came from heaven to Cain, and said unto him, "Where is Abel thy brother?"

17 Then Cain answered with a proud heart and a gruff voice, "How, O God? am I my brother's keeper?"

18 Then God said unto Cain, "Cursed be the earth that has drunk the blood of Abel thy brother; and thou, be thou trembling and shaking; and this will be a sign unto thee, that whosoever finds thee, shall kill thee."

19 But Cain wept because God had said those words to him; and Cain said unto Him "O God, whosoever finds me shall kill me, and I shall be blotted out from the face of the earth."

20 Then God said unto Cain, "Whosoever shall find thee shall not kill thee;" because before this, God had been saying to Cain, "I shall forego seven punishments on him who kills Cain." For as to the word of God to Cain, "Where is thy brother?" God said it in mercy for him, to try and make him repent.

21 For if Cain had repented at that time, and had said, "O God, forgive me my sin, and the murder of my brother," God would then have forgiven him his sin.

22 And as to God saying to Cain, "Cursed be the ground that has drunk the blood of thy brother" that also, was God's mercy on Cain. For God did not curse him, but He cursed the ground; although it was not the ground that had killed Abel, and had committed iniquity.

23 For it was meet that the curse should fall upon the murderer; yet in mercy did God so manage His thoughts as that no one should know it, and turn away from Cain.

24 And He said to him, "Where is thy brother?" To which he answered and said, "I know not." Then the Creator said to him, "Be trembling and quaking."

25 Then Cain trembled and became terrified; and through this sign did God make him an example before all the creation, as the murderer of his brother. Also did God bring trembling and terror upon him, that he might see the peace in which he was at first, and see also the trembling and terror he endured at the last; so that he might humble himself before God, and repent of his sin, and seek the peace he enjoyed at first.

26 And in the word of God that said, "I will forego seven punishments on whomsoever kills Cain," God was not seeking to kill Cain with the sword, but He sought to make him die of fasting, and praying and weeping by hard rule, until the time that he was delivered from his sin.

27 And the seven punishments are the seven generations during which God awaited Cain for the murder of his brother.

28 But as to Cain, ever since he had killed his brother, he could find no rest in any place; but went back to Adam and Eve, trembling, terrified, and defiled with blood. . . .

THE SECOND BOOK OF

[111]

Adam and Eve

CHAP. I.

The grief stricken family. Cain marries Luluwa and they move away.

WHEN Luluwa heard Cain's words, she wept and went to her father and mother, and told them how that Cain had killed his brother Abel.

2 Then they all cried aloud and lifted up their voices, and slapped their faces, and threw dust upon their heads, and rent asunder their garments, and went out and came to the place where Abel was killed.

3 And they found him lying on the earth, killed, and beasts around him; while they wept and cried because of this just one. From his body, by reason of its purity, went forth a smell of sweet spices.

4 And Adam carried him, his tears streaming down his face; and went to the Cave of Treasures, where he laid him, and wound him up with sweet spices and myrrh.

5 And Adam and Eve continued by the burial of him in great grief a hundred and forty days. Abel was fifteen and a half years old, and Cain seventeen years and a half.

6 As for Cain, when the mourning for his brother was ended, he took his sister Luluwa and married her, without leave from his father and mother; for they could not keep him from her, by reason of their heavy heart.

7 He then went down to the bottom of the mountain, away from the garden, near to the place where he had killed his brother.

8 And in that place were many fruit trees and forest trees. His sister bare him children, who in their turn began to multiply by degrees until they filled that place.

9 But as for Adam and Eve, they came not together after Abel's funeral, for seven years. After this, however, Eve conceived; and while she was with child, Adam said to her "Come, let us take an offering and offer it up unto God, and ask Him to

give us a fair child, in whom we may find comfort, and whom we may join in marriage to Abel's sister."

10 Then they prepared an offering and brought it up to the altar, and offered it before the Lord, and began to entreat Him to accept their offering, and to give them a good offspring.

11 And God heard Adam and accepted his offering. Then, they worshipped, Adam, Eve, and their daughter, and came down to the Cave of Treasures and placed a lamp in it, to burn by night and by day, before the body of Abel.

12 Then Adam and Eve continued fasting and praying until Eve's time came that she should be delivered, when she said to Adam: "I wish to go to the cave in the rock, to bring forth in it."

13 And he said, "Go and take with thee thy daughter to wait on thee; but I will remain in this Cave of Treasures before the body of my son Abel."

14 Then Eve hearkened to Adam, and went, she and her daughter. But Adam remained by himself in the Cave of Treasures.

CHAP. II.

A third son is born to Adam and Eve.

AND Eve brought forth a son perfectly beautiful in figure and in countenance. His beauty was like that of his father Adam, yet more beautiful.

2 Then Eve was comforted when she saw him, and remained eight days in the cave; then she sent her daughter unto Adam to tell him to come and see the child and name him. But the daughter stayed in his place by the body of her brother, until Adam returned. So did she.

3 But when Adam came and saw the child's good looks, his beauty, and his perfect figure, he rejoiced over him, and was comforted for Abel. Then he named the child Seth, that means, "that God has heard my prayer, and has delivered me out of my affliction." But it means also "power and strength."

4 Then after Adam had named the child, he returned to the Cave of Treasures; and his daughter went back to her mother.

5 But Eve continued in her cave, until forty days were fulfillled, when she came to Adam, and brought with her the child and her daughter.

6 And they came to a river of water, where Adam and his daughter washed themselves, because of their sorrow for Abel; but Eve and the babe washed for purification.

7 Then they returned, and took an offering, and went to the mountain and offered it up, for the babe; and God accepted their offering, and sent His blessing upon them, and upon their son Seth; and they came back to the Cave of Treasures.

8 As for Adam, he knew not again his wife Eve, all the days of his life; neither was any more offspring born of them; but only those five, Cain, Luluwa, Abel, Aklia, and Seth alone.

9 But Seth waxed in stature and in strength; and began to fast and pray, fervently.

CHAP. III

Satan appears as a beautiful woman tempting Adam, telling him he is still a youth. "Spend thy youth in mirth and pleasure." (12) The different forms which Satan takes (15).

AS for our father Adam, at the end of seven years from the day he had been severed from his wife Eve, Satan envied him, when he saw him thus separated from her; and strove to make him live with her again.

2 Then Adam arose and went up above the Cave of Treasures; and continued to sleep there night by night. But as soon as it was light every day he came down to the cave, to pray there and to receive a blessing from it.

3 But when it was evening he went up on the roof of the cave, where he slept by himself, fearing lest Satan should overcome him. And he continued thus apart thirty-nine days.

4 Then Satan, the hater of all good, when he saw Adam thus alone, fasting and praying, appeared unto him in the form of a beautiful woman, who came and stood before him in the night of the fortieth day, and said unto him:--

[114]

5 "O Adam, from the time ye have dwelt in this cave, we have experienced great peace from you, and your prayers have reached us, and we have been comforted about you.

6 "But now, O Adam, that thou hast gone up over the roof of the cave to sleep, we have had doubts about thee, and a great sorrow has come upon us because of thy separation from Eve. Then again, when thou art on the roof of this cave, thy prayer is poured out, and thy heart wanders from side to side.

7 "But when thou wast in the cave thy prayer was like fire gathered together; it came down to us, and thou didst find rest.

8 "Then I also grieved over thy children who are severed from thee; and my sorrow is great about the murder of thy son Abel; for he was righteous; and over a righteous man every one will grieve.

9 "But I rejoiced over the birth of thy son Seth; yet after a little while I sorrowed greatly over Eve, because she is my sister. For when God sent a deep sleep over thee, and drew her out of thy side, He brought me out also with her. But He raised her by placing her with thee, while He lowered me.

10 "I rejoiced over my sister for her being with thee. But God had made me a promise before, and said, 'Grieve not; when Adam has gone up on the roof of the Cave of Treasures, and is separated from Eve his wife, I will send thee to him, thou shalt join thyself to him in marriage, and bear him five children, as Eve did bear him five.'

11 "And now, lo! God's promise to me is fulfilled; for it is He who has sent me to thee for the wedding; because if thou wed me, I shall bear thee finer and better children than those of Eve.

12 "Then again, thou art as yet but a youth; end not thy youth in this world in sorrow; but spend the days of thy youth in mirth and pleasure. For thy days are few and thy trial is great. Be strong; end thy days in this world in rejoicing. I shall take pleasure in thee, and thou shall rejoice with me in this wise, and without fear.

13 "Up, then, and fulfill the command of thy God," she then drew near to Adam, and embraced him.

14 But when Adam saw that he should be overcome by her, he prayed to God with a fervent heart to deliver him from her.

15 Then God sent His Word unto Adam, saying, "O Adam, that figure is the one that promised thee the Godhead, and majesty; he is not favourably disposed towards thee; but shows himself to thee at one time in the form of a woman; another moment, in the likeness of an angel; on another occasions, in the similitude of a serpent; and at another time, in the semblance of a god; but he does all that only to destroy thy soul.

16 "Now, therefore, O Adam, understanding thy heart, I have delivered thee many a time from his hands; in order to show thee that I am a merciful God; and that I wish thy good, and that I do not wish thy ruin."

CHAP. IV.

Adam sees the Devil in his true colors.

THEN God ordered Satan to show himself to Adam in plainly, in his own hideous form.

2 But when Adam saw him, he feared, and trembled at the sight of him.

3 And God said to Adam, "Look at this devil, and at his hideous look, and know that he it is who made thee fall from brightness into darkness, from peace and rest to toil and misery.

4 And look, O Adam, at him, who said of himself that he is God! Can God be black? Would God take the form of a woman? Is there any one stronger than God? And can He be overpowered?

5 "See, then, O Adam, and behold him bound in thy presence, in the air, unable to flee away! Therefore, I say unto thee, be not afraid of him; henceforth take care, and beware of him, in whatever he may do to thee."

6 Then God drove Satan away from before Adam, whom He strengthened, and whose heart He comforted, saying to him, "Go down to the Cave of Treasures, and separate not thyself from Eve; I will quell in you all animal lust."

7 From that hour it left Adam and Eve, and they enjoyed rest by the commandment of God. But God did not the like to any one of Adam's seed; but only to Adam and Eve.

8 Then Adam worshipped before the Lord, for having delivered him, and for having layed his passions. And he came down from above the cave, and dwelt with Eve as aforetime.

9 This ended the forty days of his separation from Eve.

CHAP. V.

The devil paints a brilliant picture for Seth to feast his thoughts upon.

AS for Seth, when he was seven years old, he knew good and evil, and was consistent in fasting and praying, and spent all his nights in entreating God for mercy and forgiveness.

2 He also fasted when bringing up his offering every day, more than his father did; for he was of a fair countenance, like unto an angel of God. He also had a good heart, preserved the finest qualities of his soul: and for this reason he brought up his offering every day.

3 And God was pleased with his offering; but He was also pleased with his purity. And he continued thus in doing the will of God, and of his father and mother, until he was seven years old.

4 After that, as he was coming down from the altar, having ended his offering, Satan appeared unto him in the form of a beautiful angel, brilliant with light; with a staff of light in his hand, himself girt about with a girdle of light.

5 He greeted Seth with a beautiful smile, and began to beguile him with fair words, saying to him, "O Seth, why abidest thou in this mountain? For it is rough, full of stones and of sand, and of trees with no good fruit on them; a wilderness without habitations and without towns; no good place to dwell in. But all is heat, weariness, and trouble."

6 He said further, "But we dwell in beautiful places, in another world than this earth. Our world is one of light and our condition is of the best; our women are handsomer than any others; and I wish thee, O Seth, to wed one of them; because I see that thou art fair to look upon, and in this land there is not one woman good enough for thee. Besides, all those who live in this world, are only five souls.

7 "But in our world there are very many men and many maidens, all more beautiful one than another. I wish, therefore, to remove thee hence, that thou mayest see my relations and be wedded to which ever thou likest.

8 "Thou shalt then abide by me and be at peace; thou shalt be filled with splendour and light, as we are.

9 "Thou shalt remain in our world. and rest from this world and the misery of it; thou shalt never again feel faint and weary; thou shalt never bring up an offering, nor sue for mercy; for thou shalt commit no more sin, nor be swayed by passions.

10 "And if thou wilt hearken to what I say, thou shalt wed one of my daughters; for with us it is no sin so to do; neither is it reckoned animal lust.

11 "For in our world we have no God; but we all are gods; we all are of the light, heavenly, powerful, strong and glorious."

CHAP. VI.

Seth's conscience helps him. He returns to Adam and Eve.

WHEN Seth heard these words he was amazed, and inclined his heart to Satan's treacherous speech, and said to him, "Saidst thou there is another world created than this; and other creatures more beautiful than the creatures that are in this world?"

2 And Satan said, "Yes; behold thou hast heard me; but I will yet praise them and their ways, in thy hearing."

3 But Seth said to him, "Thy speech has amazed me; and thy beautiful description of it all.

4 "Yet I cannot go with thee to-day; not until I have gone to my father Adam and to my mother Eve, and told them all thou hast said to me. Then if they give me leave to go with thee, I will come."

5 Again Seth said, "I am afraid of doing any thing without my father's and mother's leave, lest I perish like my brother Cain, and like my father Adam, who transgressed the commandment of God. But, behold, thou knowest this place; come, and meet me here to-morrow."

6 When Satan heard this, he said to Seth, "If thou tellest thy father Adam what I have told thee, he will not let thee come with me.

7 But hearken to me; do not tell thy father and mother what I have said to thee; but come with me to-day, to our world; where thou shalt see beautiful things and enjoy thyself there, and revel this day among my children, beholding them and taking thy fill of mirth; and rejoice ever more. Then I shall bring thee back to this place to-morrow; but if thou wouldest rather abide with me, so be it."

8 Then Seth answered, "The spirit of my father and of my mother, hangs on me; and if I hide from them one day, they will die, and God will hold me guilty of sinning against them.

9 "And except that they know I am come to this place to bring up to it my offering, they would not be separated from me one hour; neither should I go to any other place, unless they let me. But they treat me most kindly, because I come back to them quickly."

10 Then Satan said to him, "What will happen to thee if thou hide thyself from them one night, and return to them at break of day?"

11 But Seth, when he saw how he kept on talking, and that he would not leave him-ran, and went up to the altar, and spread his hands unto God, and sought deliverance from Him.

12 Then God sent His Word, and cursed Satan, who fled from Him.

13 But as for Seth, he had gone up to the altar, saying thus in his heart. "The altar is the place of offering, and God is there; a divine fire shall consume it; so shall Satan be unable to hurt me, and shall not take me away thence."

14 Then Seth came down from the altar and went to his father and mother, where he found in the way, longing to hear his voice; for he had tarried a while.

15 He then began to tell them what had befallen him from Satan, under the form of an angel.

16 But when Adam heard his account, he kissed his face, and warned him against that angel, telling him it was Satan who thus appeared to him. Then Adam took Seth, and they went to the Cave of Treasures, and rejoiced therein.

17 But from that day forth Adam and Eve never parted from him, to whatever place he might go, whether for his offering or for any thing else.

18 This sign happened to Seth, when he was nine years old.

CHAP. VII.

Seth marries Aklia. Adam lives to see grand children and great-grand-children.

WHEN our father Adam saw that Seth was of a perfect heart, he wished him to marry; lest the enemy should appear to him another time, and overcome him.

2 So Adam said to his son Seth, "I wish, O my son, that thou wed thy sister Aklia, Abel's sister, that she may bear thee children, who shall replenish the earth, according to God's promise to us.

3 "Be not afraid, O my son; there is no disgrace in it. I wish thee to marry, from fear lest the enemy overcome thee."

4 Seth, however, did not wish to marry; but in obedience to his father and mother, he said not a word.

5 So Adam married him to Aklia. And he was fifteen years old.

6 But when he was twenty years of age, he begat a son, whom he called Enos; and then begat other children than him.

7 Then Enos grew up, married, and begat Cainan.

8 Cainan also grew up, married, and begat Mahalaleel.

9 Those fathers were born during Adam's life-time, and dwelt by the Cave of Treasures.

10 Then were the days of Adam nine hundred and thirty years, and those of Mahalaleel one hundred. But Mahalaleel, when he was grown up, loved fasting, praying, and with hard labours, until the end of our father Adam's days drew near.

And, lo! toward us in a bark
Comes on an old man, hoary white with eld,
Crying, "Woe to you, wicked spirits!"

Canto III., line 70-72.

CHAP. VIII.

[121]

Adam's remarkable last words. He predicts the Flood. He exhorts his offspring to good. He reveals certain mysteries of life.

WHEN our father Adam saw that his end was near, he called his son Seth, who came to him in the Cave of Treasures, and he said unto him:--

2 "O Seth, my son bring me thy children and thy children's children, that I may shed my blessing on them ere I die."

3 When Seth heard these words from his father Adam, he went from him, shed a flood of tears over his face, and gathered together his children and his children's children, and brought them to his father Adam.

4 But when our father Adam saw them around him, he wept at having to be separated from them.

5 And when they saw him weeping, they all wept together, and fell upon his face saying, "How shalt thou be severed from us, O our father? And how shall the earth receive thee and hide thee from our eyes?" Thus did lament much, and in like words.

6 Then our father Adam blessed them all, and said to Seth, after he had blessed them:--

7 "O Seth, my son, thou knowest this world--that it is full of sorrow, and of weariness; and thou knowest all that has come upon us, from our trials in it. I therefore now command thee in these words: to keep innocency, to be pure and just, and trusting in God; and lean not to the discourses of Satan, nor to the apparitions in which he will show himself to thee.

8 But keep the commandments that I give thee this day; then give the same to thy son Enos; and let Enos give it to his son Cainan; and Cainan to his son Mahalaleel; so that this commandment abide firm among all your children.

9 "O Seth, my son, the moment I am dead take ye my body and wind it up with myrrh, aloes, and cassia, and leave me here in this Cave of Treasures in which are all these tokens which God gave us from the garden.

10 "O my son, hereafter shall a flood come and all creatures, and leave out only eight souls.

11 "But, O my son, let those whom it will leave out from among your children at that time, take my body with them out of this cave; and when they have taken it with them, let the oldest among them command his children to lay my body in a ship until the flood has been assuaged, and they come out of the ship.

12 Then they shall take my body and lay it in the middle of the earth, shortly after they have been saved from the waters of the flood.

13 "For the place where my body shall be laid, is the middle of the earth; God shall come from thence and shall save all our kindred.

14 "But now, O Seth, my son, place thyself at the head of thy people; tend them and watch over them in the fear of God; and lead them in the good way, Command them to fast unto God; and make them understand they ought not to hearken to Satan, lest he destroy them.

15 "Then, again, sever thy children and thy children's children from Cain's children; do not let them ever mix with those, nor come near them either in their words or in their deeds."

16 Then Adam let his blessing descend upon Seth, and upon his children, and upon all his children's children.

17 He then turned to his son Seth, and to Eve his wife, and said to them, "Preserve this gold, this incense, and this myrrh, that God has given us for a sign; for in days that are coming, a flood will overwhelm the whole creation. But those who shall go into the ark shall take with them the gold, the incense, and the myrrh, together with my body; and will lay the gold, the incense, and the myrrh, with my body in the midst of the earth.

18 "Then, after a long time, the city in which the gold, the incense, and the myrrh are found with my body, shall be plundered. But when it is spoiled, the gold the incense, and the myrrh shall be taken care of with the spoil that is kept; and naught of them shall perish, until the Word of God, made man shall come; when kings shall take them, and shall offer to Him, gold in token of His being King; incense, in token of His being God of heaven and earth; and myrrh, in token of His passion.

19 "Cold also, as a token of His overcoming Satan, and all our foes; incense as a token that He will rise from the dead, and be exalted above things in heaven and

things in the earth; and myrrh, in token that He will drink bitter gall; and feel the pains of hell from Satan.

20 "And now, O Seth, my son, behold I have revealed unto thee hidden mysteries, which God had revealed unto me. Keep my commandment, for thyself, and for thy people,"

CHAP. IX.

 The death of Adam.

WHEN Adam had ended his commandment to Seth, his limbs were loosened, his hands and feet lost all power, his mouth became dumb, and his tongue ceased altogether to speak. He closed his eyes and gave up the ghost.

2 But when his children saw that he was dead, they threw themselves over him, men and women, old and young, weeping.

3 The death of Adam took place at the end of nine hundred and thirty years that be lived upon the earth; on the fifteenth day of Barmudeh, after the reckoning of an epact of the sun, at the ninth hour.

4 It was on a Friday, the very day on which be was created, and on which he rested; and the hour at which he died, was the same as that at which he came out of the garden.

5 Then Seth wound him up well, and embalmed him with plenty of sweet spices, from sacred trees and from the Holy Mountain; and be laid his body on the eastern side of the inside of the cave, the side of the incense; and placed in front of him a lamp-stand kept burning.

6 Then his children stood before him weeping and wailing over him the whole night until break of day.

7 Then Seth and big son Enos, and Cainan, the son of Enos, went out and took good offerings to present unto the Lord, and they came to the altar upon which Adam offered gifts to God, when he did offer.

8 But Eve said to them "Wait until we have first asked God to accept our offering, and to keep by Him the Soul of Adam His servant, and to take it up to rest."

9 And they all stood up an prayed.

CHAP. X.

"Adam was the first...."

AND when they had ended their prayer, the Word of God came and comforted them concerning their father Adam.

2 After this, they offered their gifts for themselves and for their father.

3 And when they had ended their offering, the Word of God came to Seth, the eldest among them, saying unto him, "O Seth, Seth, Seth, three times. As I was with thy father, so also shall I be with thee, until the fulfillment of the promise I made him-thy father saying, I will send My Word and save thee and thy seed.

4 But as to thy father Adam, keep thou the commandment he gave thee; and sever thy seed from that of Cain thy brother."

5 And God withdrew His Word from Seth.

6 Then Seth, Eve, and their children, came down from the mountain to the Cave of Treasures.

7 But Adam was the first whose soul died in the land of Eden, in the Cave of Treasures; for no one died before him, but his son Abel, who died murdered.

8 Then all the children of Adam rose up, and wept over their father Adam, and made offerings to him, one hundred and forty days.

CHAP. XI.

Seth becomes head of the most happy and just tribe of people who ever lived.

AFTER the death of Adam and of Eve, Seth severed his children, and his children's children, from Cain's children. Cain and his seed went down and dwelt westward, below the place where he had killed his brother Abel.

2 But Seth and his children, dwelt northwards upon the mountain of the Cave of Treasures, in order to be near to their father Adam.

3 And Seth the elder, tall and good, with a fine soul, and of a strong mind, stood at the head of his people; and tended them in innocence, penitence, and meekness, and did not allow one of them to go down to Cain's children.

4 But because of their own purity, they were named "Children of God," and they were with God, instead of the hosts of angels who fell; for they continued in praises to God, and in singing psalms unto Him, in their cave--the Cave of Treasures.

5 Then Seth stood before the body of his father Adam, and of his mother Eve, and prayed night and day, and asked for mercy towards himself and his children; and that when he had some difficult dealing with a child, He would give him counsel.

6 But Seth and his children did not like earthly work, but gave themselves to heavenly things; for they had no other thought than praises, doxologies, and psalms unto God.

7 Therefore did they at all times hear the voices of angels, praising and glorifying God; from within the garden, or when they were sent by God on an errand, or when they were going up to heaven.

8 For Seth and his children, by reason of their own purity, heard and saw those angels. Then, again, the garden was not far above them, but only some fifteen spiritual cubits.

9 Now one spiritual cubit answers to three cubits of man, altogether forty-five cubits.

10 Seth and his children dwelt on the mountain below the garden; they sowed not, neither did they reap; they wrought no food for the body. not even wheat; but only offerings. They ate of the fruit and of trees well flavoured that grew on the mountain where they dwelt.

11 Then Seth often fasted every forty days, as did also his eldest children. For the family of Seth smelled the smell of the trees in the garden, when the wind blew that way.

12 They were happy, innocent, without sudden fear, there was no jealousy, no evil action, no hatred among them. There was no animal passion; from no mouth among them went forth either foul words or curse; neither evil counsel nor fraud. For the men of that time never swore, but under hard circumstances, when men must swear, they swore by the blood of Abel the just.

13 But they constrained their children and their women every day in the cave to fast and pray, and to worship the most High God. They blessed themselves n the body of their father Adam, and anointed themselves with it.

14 And they did so until the end of Seth drew near.

CHAP. XII.

 Seth's family affairs. His death. The headship of Enos. How the outcast branch of Adam's family fared.

THEN Seth, the just, called his son Enos, and Cainan, son of Enos, and Mahalaleel, son of Cainan, and said unto them:--

2 "As my end is near, I wish to build a roof over the altar on which gifts are offered."

3 They hearkened to his commandment and went out, all of them, both old and young, and worked hard at it, and built a beautiful roof over the altar.

4 And Seth's thought in so doing, was that a blessing should come upon his children on the mountain; and that he should present an offering for them before his death.

5 Then when the building of the roof was completed, he commanded them to make offerings. They worked diligently at these, and brought them to Seth their father who took them and offered them upon the altar; and prayed God to accept their offerings, to have mercy on the souls of his children, and to keep them from the hand of Satan.

6 And God accepted his offering, and sent His blessing upon him and upon his children. And then God made a promise to Seth, saying, "At the end of the great five days and a half, concerning which I have made a promise to thee and to thy father, I will send My Word and save thee and thy seed."

7 Then Seth and his children, and his children's children, met together, and came down from the altar, and went to the Cave of Treasures--where they prayed, and blessed themselves in the body of our father Adam, and anointed themselves with it.

8 But Seth abode in the Cave of Treasures, a few days, and then suffered--sufferings unto death.

9 Then Enos, his first-born son, came to him, with Cainan, his son, and Mahalaleel, Cainan's son, and Jared, the son of Mahalaleel, and Enoch, Jared's son, with their wives and children to receive a blessing from Seth.

10 Then Seth prayed over them, and blessed them, and adjured them by the blood of Abel the just, saying, "I beg of you, my children, not to let one of you go down from this Holy and pure Mountain.

11 Make no fellowship with the children of Cain the murderer and the sinner, who killed his brother; for ye know, O my children, that we flee from him, and from all his sin with all our might because he killed his brother Abel."

12 After having said this, Seth blessed Enos, his first-born son, and commanded him habitually to minister in purity before the body of our father Adam, all the days of his life; then, also, to go at times to the altar which he Seth had built. And he commanded him to feed his people in righteousness, in judgment and purity all the days of his life.

13 Then the limbs of Seth were loosened; his hands and feet lost all power; his mouth became dumb and unable to speak; and he gave up the ghost and died the day after his nine hundred and twelfth year; on the twenty-seventh day of the month Abib; Enoch being then twenty years old.

14 Then they wound up the body of Seth, and embalmed him with sweet spices, and laid him in the Cave of Treasures, on the right side of our father Adam's body, and they mourned for him forty days. They offered gifts for him, as they had done for our father Adam.

15 After the death of Seth Enos rose at the head of his people, whom he fed in righteousness, and judgment, as his father had commanded him.

16 But by the time Enos was eight hundred and twenty years old, Cain had a large progeny; for they married frequently, being given to animal lusts; until the land below the mountain, was filled with them.

CHAP. XIII.

"Among the children of Cain there was much robbery, murder and sin."

IN those days lived Lamech the blind, who was of the sons of Cain. He had a son whose name was Atun, and they two had much cattle.

2 But Lamech was in the habit of sending them to feed with a young shepherd, who tended them; and who, when coming home in the evening wept before his grandfather, and before his father Atun and his mother Hazina, and said to them, "As for me, I cannot feed those cattle alone, lest one rob me of some of them, or kill me for the sake of them." For among the children of Cain, there was much robbery, murder, and sin.

3 Then Lamech pitied him, and he said, "Truly, he when alone, might be overpowered by the men of this place."

4 So Lamech arose, took a bow he had kept ever since he was a youth, ere he became blind, and he took large arrows, and smooth stones, and a sling which he had, and went to the field with the young shepherd, and placed himself behind the cattle; while the young shepherd watched the cattle. Thus did Lamech many days.

5 Meanwhile Cain, ever since God had cast him off, and had cursed him with trembling and terror, could neither settle nor find rest in any one place; but wandered from place to place.

6 In his wanderings he came to Lamech's wives, and asked them about him. They said to him, "He is in the field with the cattle."

7 Then Cain went to look for him; and as he came into the field, the young shepherd heard the noise he made, and the cattle herding together from before him.

8 Then said he to Lamech, "O my lord, is that a wild beast or a robber?"

9 And Lamech said to him, "Make me understand which way he looks, when he comes up."

10 Then Lamech bent his bow, placed an arrow on it, and fitted a stone in the sling, and when Cain came out from the open country, the shepherd said to Lamech, "Shoot, behold, he is coming."

11 Then Lamech shot at Cain with his arrow and hit him in his side. And Lamech struck him with a stone from his sling, that fell upon his face, and knocked out both his eyes; then Cain fell at once and died.

12 Then Lamech and the young shepherd came up to him, and found him lying on the ground. And the young shepherd said to him, "It is Cain our grandfather, whom thou hast killed, O my lord!"

13 Then was Lamech sorry for it, and from the bitterness of his regret, he clapped his hands together, and struck with his flat palm the head of the youth, who fell as if dead; but Lamech thought it was a feint; so he took up a stone and smote him, and smashed his head until he died.

CHAP. XIV.

Time, like an ever-rolling stream, bears away another generation of men.

WHEN Enos was nine hundred years old, all the children of Seth, and of Cainan, and his first-born, with their wives and children, gathered around him, asking for a blessing from him.

2 He then prayed over them and blessed them, and adjured them by the blood of Abel the just saying to them, "Let not one of your children go down from this Holy Mountain, and let them make no fellowship with the children of Cain the murderer."

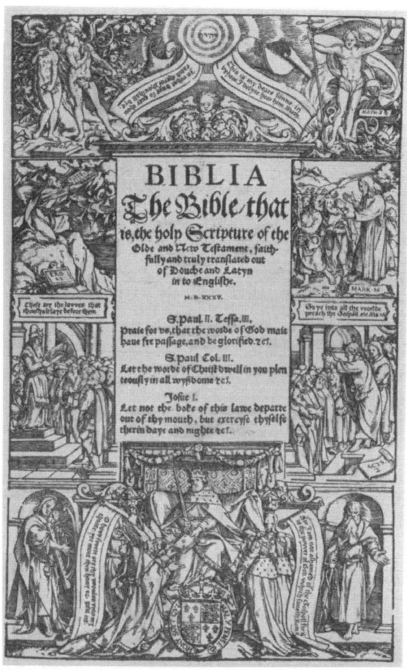

FACSIMILE OF ACTUAL PAGE OF ORIGINAL GUTENBERG BIBLE.

The first successful printing was done in 1450 A.D. when Gutenberg printed the Old Testament in Latin. There are about 45 copies of the precious Gutenberg

[131]

Bible in existence that have survived the chances of Europe and its wars for five hundred years.

3 Then Enos called his son Cainan and said to him, "See, O my son, and set thy heart on thy people, and establish them in righteousness, and in innocence; and stand ministering before the body of our father Adam, all the days of thy life."

4 After this Enos entered into rest, aged nine hundred and eighty-five years; and Cainan wound him up, and laid him in the Cave of Treasures on the left of his father Adam; and made offerings for him, after the custom of his fathers.

CHAP. XV.

The offspring of Adam continue to keep the Cave of Treasures as a family shrine.

AFTER the death of Enos, Cainan stood at the head of his people in righteousness and innocence, as his father had commanded him; he also continued to minister before the body of Adam, inside the Cave of Treasures.

2 Then when he had lived nine hundred and ten years, suffering and affliction came upon him. And when he was about to enter into rest, all the fathers with their wives and children came to him, and he blessed them, and adjured them by the blood of Abel, the just, saying to them, "Let not one among you go down from this Holy Mountain; and make no fellowship with the children of Cain the murderer."

3 Mahalaleel, his first-born son, received this commandment from his father, who blessed him and died.

4 Then Mahalaleel embalmed him with sweet spices, and laid him in the Cave of Treasures, with his fathers; and they made offerings for him, after the custom of their fathers.

CHAP. XVI.

The good branch of the family is still afraid of the children of Cain.

THEN Mahalaleel stood over his people, and fed them in righteousness and innocence, and watched them to see they held no intercourse with the children of Cain.

2 He also continued in the Cave of Treasures praying and ministering before the body of our father Adam, asking God for mercy on himself and on his people; until he was eight hundred and seventy years old, when he fell sick.

3 Then all his children gathered unto him, to see him, and to ask for his blessing on them all, ere he left this world.

4 Then Mahalaleel arose and sat on his bed, his tears streaming down his face, and he called his eldest son Jared, who came to him.

5 He then kissed his face, and said to him, "O Jared, my son, I adjure thee by Him who made heaven and earth, to watch over thy people, and to feed them in righteousness and in innocence; and not to let one of them go down from this Holy Mountain to the children of Cain, lest he perish with them.

6 "Hear, O my son, hereafter there shall come a great destruction upon this earth on account of them; God will be angry with the world, and will destroy them with waters.

7 "But I also know that thy children will not hearken to thee, and that they will go down from this mountain and hold intercourse with the children of Cain, and that they shall perish with them.

8 "O my son! teach them, and watch over them, that no guilt attach to thee on their account."

9 Mahalaleel said, moreover, to his son Jared, "When I die, embalm my body and lay it in the Cave of Treasures, by the bodies of my fathers; then stand thou by my body and pray to God; and take care of them, and fulfill thy ministry before them, until thou enterest into rest thyself."

10 Mahalaleel then blessed all his children; and then lay down on his bed, and entered into rest like his fathers.

11 But when Jared saw that his father Mahalaleel was dead, he wept, and sorrowed, and embraced and kissed his hands and his feet; and so did all his children.

12 And his children embalmed him carefully, and laid him by the bodies of his fathers. Then they arose, and mourned for him forty days.

CHAP. XVII.

Jared turns martinet. He is lured away to the land of Cain where he sees many voluptuous sights. Jared barely escapes with a clean heart.

THEN Jared kept his father's commandment, and arose like a lion over his people. He fed them in righteousness and innocence, and commanded them to do nothing without his counsel. For he was afraid concerning them, lest they should go to the children of Cain.

2 Wherefore did he give them orders repeatedly; and continued to do so until the end of the four hundred and eighty-fifth year of his life.

3 At the end of these said years, there came unto him this sign. As Jared was standing like a lion before the bodies of his fathers, praying and warning his people, Satan envied him, and wrought a beautiful apparition, because Jared would not let his children do aught without his counsel.

4 Satan then appeared to him with thirty men of his hosts, in the form of handsome men; Satan himself being the elder and tallest among them, with a fine beard.

5 They stood at the mouth of the cave, and called out Jared, from within it.

6 He came out to them, and found them looking like fine men, full of light, and of great beauty. He wondered at their beauty and at their looks; and thought within himself whether they might not be of the children of Cain.

7 He said also in his heart, "As the children of Cain cannot come up to the height of this mountain, and none of them is so handsome as these appear to be; and among these men there is not one of my kindred--they must be strangers."

8 Then Jared and they exchanged a greeting and he said to the elder among them, "O my father, explain to me the wonder that is in thee, and tell me who these are, with thee; for they look to me like strange men."

9 Then the elder began to weep, and the rest wept with him; and he said to Jared: "I am Adam whom God made first; and this is Abel my son, who was killed by his brother Cain, into whose heart Satan put to murder him.

10 "Then this is my son Seth, whom I asked of the Lord, who gave him to me, to comfort me instead of Abel.

11 "Then this one is my son Enos, son of Seth, and that other one is Cainan, son of Enos, and that other one is Mahalaleel, son of Cainan, thy father."

12 But Jared remained wondering at their appearance, and at the speech of the elder to him.

13 Then the elder said to him, "Marvel not, O my son; we live in the land north of the garden, which God created before the world. He would not let us live there, but placed us inside the garden, below which ye are now dwelling.

14 "But after that I transgressed, He made me come out of it, and I was left to dwell in this cave; great and sore troubles came upon me; and when my death drew near, I commanded my son Seth to tend his people well; and this my commandment is to be handed from one to another, unto the end of the generations to come.

15 "But, O Jared, my son, we live in beautiful regions, while you live here in misery, as this thy father Mahalaleel informed me; telling me that a great flood will come and overwhelm the whole earth.

16 "Therefore, O my son, fearing for your sakes, I rose and took my children with me, and came hither for us to visit thee and thy children; but I found thee standing in this cave weeping, and thy children scattered about this mountain, in the heat and in misery.

17 "But, O my son, as we missed our way, and came as far as this, we found other men below this mountain; who inhabit a beautiful country, full of trees and of fruits, and of all manner of verdure; it is like a garden; so that when we found them we thought they were you; until thy father Mahalaleel told me they were no such thing.

18 "Now, therefore, O my son, hearken to my counsel, and go down to them, thou and thy children. Ye will rest from all this suffering in which ye are. But if thou wilt not go down to them, then, arise, take thy children, and come with us to our

garden; ye shall live in our beautiful land, and ye shall rest from all this trouble, which thou and thy children are now bearing."

19 But Jared when he heard this discourse from the elder, wondered; and went hither and thither, but at that moment he found not one of his children.

20 Then he answered and said to the elder, "Why have you hidden yourselves until this day?"

21 And the elder replied, "If thy father had not told us, we should not have known it."

22 Then Jared believed his words were true.

23 So that elder said to Jared, "Wherefore didst thou turn about, so and so?" And he said, "I was seeking one of my children, to tell him about my going with you, and about their coming down to those about whom thou hast spoken to me."

24 When the elder heard Jared's intention, he said to him, "Let alone that purpose at present, and come with us; thou shalt see our country; if the land in which we dwell pleases thee, we and thou shall return hither and take thy family with us. But if our country does not please thee, thou shalt come back to thine own place."

25 And the elder urged Jared, to go before one of his children came to counsel him otherwise.

26 Jared, then, came out of the cave and went with them, and among them. And they comforted him, until they came to the top of the mountain of the sons of Cain.

27 Then said the elder to one of his companions, "We have forgotten something by the mouth of the cave, and that is the chosen garment we had brought to clothe Jared withal."

28 He then said to one of them, "Go back, thou, some one; and we will wait for thee here, until thou come back. Then will we clothe Jared and he shall be like us, good, handsome, and fit to come with us into our country."

29 Then that one went back.

30 But when he was a short distance off, the elder called to him and said to him, "Tarry thou, until I come up and speak to thee."

31 Then he stood still, and the elder went up to him and said to him, "One thing we forgot at the cave, it is this--to put out the lamp that burns inside it, above the bodies that are therein. Then come back to us, quick."

32 That one went, and the elder came back to his fellows and to Jared. And they came down from the mountain, and Jared with them; and they stayed by a fountain of water, near the houses of the children of Cain, and waited for their companion until he brought the garment for Jared.

33 He, then, who went, back to the cave, put out the lamp, and came to them and brought a phantom with him and showed it them. And when Jared saw it he wondered at the beauty and grace thereof, and rejoiced in his heart believing it was all true.

34 But while they were staying there, three of them went into houses of the sons of Cain, and said to them, "Bring us to-day some food by the fountain of water, for us and our companions to eat."

35 But when the sons of Cain saw them, they wondered at them and thought: "These are beautiful to look at, and such as we never saw before." So they rose and came with them to the fountain of water, to see their companions.

36 They found them so very handsome, that they cried aloud about their places for others to gather together and come and look at these beautiful beings. Then they gathered around them both men and women.

37 Then the elder said to them, "We are strangers in your land, bring us some good food and drink you and your women, to refresh ourselves with you."

38 When those men heard these words of the elder, every one of Cain's sons brought his wife, and another brought his daughter, and so, many women came to them; every one addressing Jared either for himself or for his wife; all alike.

39 But when Jared saw what they did, his very soul wrenched itself from them; neither would he taste of their food or of their drink.

40 The elder saw hint as he wrenched himself from them, and said to him, "Be not sad; I am the great elder, as thou shalt see me do, do thyself in like manner."

41 Then he spread his hands and took one of the women, and five of his companions did the same before Jared, that he should do as they did.

42 But when Jared saw them working infamy he wept, and said in his mind,--My fathers never did the like.

43 He then spread his hands and prayed with a fervent heart, and with much weeping, and entreated God to deliver him from their hands.

44 No sooner did Jared begin to pray than the elder fled with his companions; for they could not abide in a place of prayer.

45 Then Jared turned round but could not see them, but found himself standing in the midst of the children of Cain.

46 He then wept and said, "O God, destroy me not with this race, concerning which my fathers have warned me; for now, O my Lord God, I was thinking that those who appeared unto me were my fathers; but I have found them out to be devils, who allured me by this beautiful apparition, until I believed them.

47 "But now I ask Thee, O God, to deliver me from this race, among whom I am now
staying, as Thou didst deliver me from those devils. Send Thy angel to draw me out of the midst of them; for I have not myself power to escape from among them."

48 When Jared had ended his prayer, God sent His angel in the midst of them, who took Jared and set him upon the mountain, and showed him the way, gave him counsel, and then departed from him.

CHAP. XVIII.

 Confusion in the Cave of Treasures. Miraculous speech of the dead Adam.

THE children of Jared were in the habit of visiting him hour after hour, to receive his blessing and to ask his advice for every thing they did; and when he had a work to do, they did it for him.

2 But this time when they went into the cave they found not Jared, but they found the lamp put out, and the bodies of the fathers thrown about, and voices came from them by the power of God, that said, "Satan in an apparition has deceived our son, wishing to destroy him, as he destroyed our son Cain."

3 They said also, "Lord God of heaven and earth, deliver our son from the hand of Satan, who wrought a great and false apparition before him," They also spake of other matters, by the power of God.

4 But when the children of Jared heard these voices they feared, and stood weeping for their father; for they knew not what had befallen him.

5 And they wept for him that day until the setting of the sun.

6 Then came Jared with a woeful countenance, wretched in mind and body, and sorrowful at having been separated from the bodies of his fathers.

7 But as he was drawing near to the cave, his children saw him, and hastened to the cave, and hung upon his neck, crying, and saying to him, "O father, where hast thou been, and why hast thou left us, as thou wast not wont to do?" And again, "O father, when thou didst disappear, the lamp over the bodies of our fathers went out, the bodies were thrown about, and voices came from them."

8 When Jared heard this he was sorry, and went into the cave; and there found the bodies thrown about, the lamp put out, and the fathers themselves praying for his deliverance from the hand of Satan.

9 Then Jared fell upon the bodies and embraced them, and said, "O my fathers, through your intercession, let God deliver me from the hand of Satan! And I beg you will ask God to keep me and to bide me from him unto the day of my death."

10 Then all the voices ceased save the voice of our father Adam, who spake to Jared by the power of God, just as one would speak to his fellow, saying, "O Jared, my son, offer gifts to God for having delivered thee from the hand of Satan; and when thou bringest those offerings, so be it that thou offerest them on the altar on which I did offer. Then also, beware of Satan; for he deluded me many a time with his apparitions, wishing to destroy me, but God delivered me out of his hand.

11 "Command thy people that they be on their guard against him; and never cease to offer up gifts to God."

12 Then the voice of Adam also became silent; and Jared and his children wondered at this. Then they laid the bodies as they were it first; and Jared and his children stood praying the whole of that night, until break of day.

13 Then Jared made an offering and offered it up on the altar, as Adam had commanded him. And as he went up to the altar, he prayed to God for mercy and for forgiveness of his sin, concerning the lamp going out.

14 Then God appeared unto Jared on the altar and blessed him and his children, and accepted their offerings; and commanded Jared to take of the sacred fire from the altar, and with it to light the lamp that shed light on the body of Adam.

CHAP. XIX.

 The children of Jared are led astray.

THEN God revealed to him again the promise He had made to Adam; He explained to him the 5500 years, and revealed unto him the mystery of His coming upon the earth.

2 And God said to Jared, "As to that fire which thou hast taken from the altar to light the lamp withal, let it abide with you to give light to the bodies; and let it not come out of the cave, until the body of Adam comes out of it.

3 But, O Jared, take care of the fire, that it burn bright in the lamp; neither go thou again out of the cave, until thou receivest an order through a vision, and not in an apparition, when seen by thee.

4 "Then command again thy people not to hold intercourse with the children of Cain, and not to learn their ways; for I am God who loves not hatred and works of iniquity."

5 God gave also many other commandments to Jared, and blessed him. And then withdrew His Word from him.

6 Then Jared drew near with his children, took some fire, and came down to the cave, and lighted the lamp before the body of Adam; and he gave his people commandments as God had told him to do.

7 This sign happened to Jared at the end of his four hundred and fiftieth year; as did also many other wonders, we do not record. But we record only this one for shortness sake, and in order not to lengthen our narrative.

8 And Jared continued to teach his children eighty years; but after that they began to transgress the commandments he had given them, and to do many things without his counsel. They began to go down from the Holy Mountain one after another, and to mix with the children of Cain, in foul fellowships.

9 Now the reason for which the children of Jared went down the Holy Mountain, is this, that we will now reveal unto you.

CHAP. XX.

Ravishing music; strong drink loosed among the sons of Cain. They don colorful clothing. The children of Seth look on with longing eyes. They revolt from wise counsel; they descend the mountain into the valley of iniquity. They can not ascend the mountain again.

AFTER Cain had gone down to the land of dark soil, and his children had multiplied therein, there was one of them, whose name was Genun, son of Lamech the blind who slew Cain.

2 But as to this Genun, Satan came into him in his childhood; and he made sundry trumpets and horns, and string instruments, cymbals and psalteries, and lyres and harps, and flutes; and he played on them at all times and at every hour.

3 And when he played on them, Satan came into them, so that from among them were heard beautiful and sweet sounds, that ravished the heart.

4 Then he gathered companies upon companies to play on them; and when they played, it pleased well the children of Cain, who inflamed themselves with sin among themselves, and burnt as with fire; while Satan inflamed their hearts, one with another, and increased lust among them.

5 Satan also taught Genun to bring strong drink out of com; and this Genun used to bring together companies upon companies in drink-houses; and brought into their hands all manner of fruits and flowers; and they drank together.

6 Thus did this Genun multiply sin exceedingly; he also acted with pride, and taught the children of Cain to commit all manner of the grossest wickedness, which they knew not; and put them up to manifold doings which they knew not before.

7 Then Satan, when he saw that they yielded to Genun and hearkened to him in every thing he told them, rejoiced greatly, increased Genun's understanding, until he took iron and with it made weapons of war.

8 Then when they were drunk, hatred and murder increased among them; one man used violence against another to teach him evil taking his children and defiling them before him.

9 And when men saw they were overcome, and saw others that were not overpowered, those who were beaten came to Genun, took refuge with him, and he made them his confederates.

10 Then sin increased among them greatly; until a man married his own sister, or daughter, or mother, and others; or the daughter of his father's sister, so that there was no more distinction of relationship, and they no longer knew what is iniquity; but did wickedly, and the earth was defiled with sin, and they angered God the Judge, who had created them.

11 But Genun gathered together companies upon companies, that played on horns and on all the other instruments we have already mentioned, at the foot of the Holy Mountain; and they did so in order that the children of Seth who were on the Holy Mountain should hear it.

12 But when the children of Seth heard the noise, they wondered, and came by companies, and stood on the top of the mountain to look at those below; and they did thus a whole year.

13 When, at the end of that year, Genun saw that they were being won over to him little by little, Satan entered into him, and taught him to make dyeing-stuffs for garments of divers patterns, and made him understand how to dye crimson and purple and what not.

14 And the sons of Cain who wrought all this, and shone in beauty and gorgeous apparel, gathered together at the foot of the mountain in splendour, with horns and gorgeous dresses, and horse races, committing all manner of abominations.

[142]

15 Meanwhile the children of Seth, who were on the Holy Mountain, prayed and praised God, in the place of the hosts of angels who had fallen; wherefore God had called them "angels," because He rejoiced over them greatly.

16 But after this, they no longer kept His commandment, nor held by the promise He had made to their fathers; but they relaxed from their fasting and praying, and from the counsel of Jared their father. And they kept on gathering together on the top of the mountain, to look upon the children of Cain, from morning until evening, and upon what they did, upon their beautiful dresses and ornaments.

17 Then the children of Cain looked up from below, and saw the children of Seth, standing in troops on the top of the mountain; and they called to them to come down to them.

18 But the children of Seth said to them from above, "We don't know the way." Then Genun, the son of Lamech, heard them say they did not know the way, and he bethought himself how he might bring them down.

19 Then Satan appeared to him by night, saying, "There is no way for them to come down from the mountain on which they dwell; but when they come to-morrow, say to them, 'Come ye to the western side of the mountain; there you will find the way of a stream of water, that comes down to the foot of the mountain, between two hills; come down that way to us.'"

20 Then when it was day, Genun blew the horns and beat the drums below the mountain, as he was wont. The children of Seth heard it, and came as they used to do.

21 Then Genun said to them from down below, "Go to the western side of the mountain, there you will find the way to come down."

22 But when the children of Seth heard these words from him, they went back into the cave to Jared, to tell him all they had heard.

23 Then when Jared heard it, he was grieved; for he knew that they would transgress his counsel.

24 After this a hundred men of the children of Seth gathered together, and said among themselves, "Come, let us go down to the children of Cain, and see what they do, and enjoy ourselves with them."

25 But when Jared heard this of the hundred men, his very soul was moved, and his heart was grieved. He then arose with great fervour, and stood in the midst of them, and adjured them by the blood of Abel the just, "Let not one of you go down from this holy and pure mountain, in which our fathers have ordered its to dwell."

26 But when Jared saw that they did not receive his words, he said unto them, "O my good and innocent and holy children, know that when once you go down from this holy mountain, God will not allow you to return again to it."

27 He again adjured them, saying, "I adjure by the death of our father Adam, and by the blood of Abel, of Seth, of Enos, of Cainan, and of Mahalaleel, to hearken to me, and not to go down from this holy mountain; for the moment you leave it, you will be reft of life and of mercy; and you shall no longer be called 'children of God,' but 'children of the devil.'"

28 But they would not hearken to his words.

29 Enoch at that time was already grown up, and in his zeal for God, be arose and said, "Hear me, O ye sons of Seth, small and great--when ye transgress the commandment of our fathers, and go down from this holy mountain--ye shall not come up hither again for ever."

30 But they rose up against Enoch, and would not hearken to his words, but went down from the Holy Mountain.

31 And when they looked at the daughters of Cain, at their beautiful figures, and at their hands and feet dyed with colour, and tattooed in ornaments on their faces, the fire of sin was kindled in them.

32 Then Satan made them look most beautiful before the sons of Seth, as he also made the sons of Seth appear of the fairest in the eyes of the daughters of Cain, so that the daughters of Cain lusted after the sons of

Seth like ravenous beasts, and the sons of Seth after the daughters of Cain, until they committed abomination with them.

33 But after they had thus fallen into this defilement, they returned by the way they had come, and tried to ascend the Holy Mountain. But they could not,

because the stones of that holy mountain were of fire flashing before them, by reason of which they could not go up again.

34 And God was angry with them, and repented of them because they had come down from glory, and had thereby lost or forsaken their own purity or innocence, and were fallen into the defilement of sin.

35 Then God sent His Word to Jared, saying, "These thy children, whom thou didst call 'My children,'--behold they have transgressed My commandment, and have gone down to the abode of perdition, and of sin. Send a messenger to those that are left, that they may not go down, and be lost."

36 Then Jared wept before the Lord, and asked of Him mercy and forgiveness. But he wished that his soul might depart from his body, rather than hear these words from God about the going down of his children from the Holy Mountain.

37 But he followed God's order, and preached unto them not to go down from that holy mountain, and not to hold intercourse with the children of Cain.

38 But they heeded not his message, and would not obey his counsel.

CHAP. XXI.

Jared dies in sorrow for his sons who had gone astray. A prediction of the Flood.

AFTER this another company gathered together, and they went to look after their brethren; but they perished as well as they. And so it was, company after company, until only a few of them were left.

2 Then Jared sickened from grief, and his sickness was such that the day of his death drew near.

3 Then he called Enoch his eldest son, and Methuselah Enoch's son, and Lamech the son of Methuselah, and Noah the son of Lamech.

4 And when they were come to him he prayed over them and blessed them, and said to them, "Ye are righteous, innocent sons; go ye not down from this holy mountain; for behold, your children and your children's children have gone down from this holy mountain, and have estranged themselves from this holy mountain, through their abominable lust and transgression of God's commandment.

5 "But I know, through the power of God, that He will not leave you on this holy mountain, because your children have transgressed His commandment and that of our fathers, which we had received from them.

6 "But, O my sons, God will take you to a strange land, and ye never shall again return to behold with your eyes this garden and this holy mountain.

7 "Therefore, O my sons, set your hearts on your own selves, and keep the commandment of God which is with you. And when you go from this holy mountain, into a strange land which ye know not, take with you the body of our father Adam, and with it these three precious, gifts and offerings, namely, the gold, the incense, and the myrrh; and let them be in the place where the body of our father Adam shall lay.

8 "And unto him of you who shall be left, O my sons, shall the Word of God come, and
when he goes out of this land he shall take with him the body of our father Adam, and shall lay it in the middle of the earth the place in which salvation shall be wrought."

9 Then Noah said unto him, "Who is he of us that shall be left?"

10 And Jared answered, "Thou art he that shall be left. And thou shalt take the body of our father Adam from the cave, and place it with thee in the ark when the flood comes.

11 "And thy son Shem, who shall come out of thy loins, he it is who shall lay the body of our father Adam in the middle of the earth, in the place whence salvation shall come."

12 Then Jared turned to his son Enoch, and said unto him, "Thou, my son, abide in this cave, and minister diligently before the body of our father Adam all the days of thy life; and feed thy people in righteousness and innocence."

13 And Jared said no more. His hands were loosened, his eyes closed, and he entered into rest like his fathers. His death took place in the three hundred and sixtieth year of Noah, and in the nine hundred and eighty-ninth year of his own life; on the twelfth of Takhsas on a Friday.

14 But as Jared died, tears streamed down his face by reason of his great sorrow, for the children of Seth, who had fallen in his days.

15 Then Enoch, Methuselah, Lamech and Noah, these four, wept over him; embalmed him carefully, and then laid him in the Cave of Treasures. Then they rose and mourned for him forty days.

16 And when these days of mourning were ended, Enoch, Methuselah, Lamech and Noah remained in sorrow of heart, because their father had departed from them, and they saw him no more.

CHAP. XXII.

THE DELUGE.

 Only three righteous men left in the world. The evil conditions of men prior to the Flood.

BUT Enoch kept the commandment of Jared his father, and continued to minister in the cave.

2 It is this Enoch to whom many wonders happened, and who also wrote a celebrated book; but those wonders may not be told in this place.

[148]

3 Then after this, the children of Seth went astray and fell, they, their children and their wives. And when Enoch, Methuselah, Lamech and Noah saw them, their hearts suffered by reason of their fall into doubt full of unbelief; and they wept and sought of God mercy, to preserve them, and to bring them out of that wicked generation.

4 Enoch continued in his ministry before the Lord three hundred and eighty-five years, and at the end of that time he became aware through the grace of God, that God intended to remove him from the earth.

5 He then said to his son, "O my son, I know that God intends to bring the waters of the Flood upon the earth, and to destroy our creation.

6 "And ye are the last rulers over this people on this mountain; for I know that not one will be left you to beget children on this holy mountain; neither shall any one of you rule over the children of his people; neither shall any great company be left of you, on this mountain."

7 Enoch said also to them, "Watch over your souls, and hold fast by your fear of God and by your service of Him, and worship Him in upright faith, and serve Him in righteousness, innocence and judgment, in repentance and also in purity."

8 When Enoch had ended his commandments to them, God transported him from that mountain to the land of life, to the mansions of the righteous and of the chosen, the abode of Paradise of joy, in light that reaches up to heaven; light that is outside the light of this world; for it is the light of God, that fills the whole world, but which no place can contain.

9 Thus, because Enoch was in the light of God, he found himself out of the reach of death; until God would have him die.

10 Altogether, not one of our fathers or of their children, remained on that holy mountain, except those three, Methuselah, Lamech, and Noah. For all the rest went down from the mountain and fell into sin with the children of Cain. Therefore were they forbidden that mountain, and none remained on it but those three men.

The End.

.

Other books published by Zuubooks.com

Stolen Legacy
ISBN: 9781451586558

The Seven Tablets of Creation: ENUMA ELISH
ISBN: 9781451586541

The Aquarian Gospel of Jesus the Christ
ISBN: 9781448682669

St. Ignatius of Loyola Spiritual Exercises
with Journal
ISBN: 9781448621859

The Complete Writings of St. Francis of Assisi with Biography
ISBN: 9781449952778

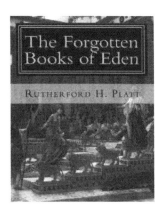

The Forgotten Books of Eden
ISBN: 9781451590791

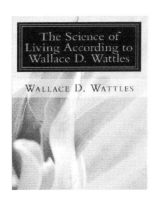

The Science of Living according to Wallace D. Wattles
Includes Wallace D. Wattles most famous works:
The Science of Getting Rich, The Science of Being Great and The Science of
Being Well
ISBN: 9781450510943

Printed in Great Britain
by Amazon.co.uk, Ltd.,
Marston Gate.